T0150984

OH GOD, I'M DYING!

"Despite facing some of the toughest challenges in life, Mark and Debbie Smith have led their ministries by loving people and by applying servant leadership principles. This book teaches you how to learn from and how to persevere in tough times!"

—**John C. Maxwell**, *New York Times* Bestselling Author and Founder of The John Maxwell Company

"Mark, thank you for turning a test into a testimony! Your mess is a message for us all! This book skillfully and sensitively presents a message that will strengthen faith, renew hope and provide spiritual guidelines that will make a difference in the lives of all who read it. I could not put it down! A page-turner!"

—**Dr. Benny Tate**, Senior Pastor, Rock Springs Church, Milner, Georgia

"Anyone who has encountered Mark Smith will testify he embraces William Carey's philosophy: 'Expect great things from God; attempt great things for God.' Mark is a formidable presence. But Mark has a secret—not one he wants to *hide*, but one he has chosen to *highlight* through this book. He is a weak and broken man whose sustaining hope and sincere boast is in the enabling grace of his Lord. There's no telling what God might do through a man who humbly and sincerely maintains that posture."

—**Ralph E. Enlow, Jr.**, Former President, Association for Biblical Higher Education

"In *Oh God, I'm Dying!*, my dear friend, Dr. Mark Smith, shares his personal story of suffering. *This book had to be written!* Its message will bring hope, encouragement and empowerment to multitudes who are experiencing the pain of brokenness: physical, emotional or otherwise. Mark's life and his God-dream of a lifetime of ministry in Christian higher education could easily have ended in a terrible car accident. The head-on collision resulted in a broken body, intense physical pain and emotional anguish; but in the dark hours when Mark was helpless and almost hopeless, he discovered the vastness of God's grace and faithfulness."

—**Doug Carter**, Senior Vice President,
EQUIP Leadership, Inc.

"We have all experienced pain during the journey of life. The pain may be physical, emotional, mental or a combination of all of these. Dr. Mark Smith's story provides each of us with evidence of God's grace. This grace gives us hope, sustains us and shows us how God can use us to love and to serve others despite the pain."

—**Mike Crapps,** President and CEO,
First Community Bank, Lexington, South Carolina

"We don't choose suffering; suffering chooses us. The question is, how should we respond to it? In *Oh God, I'm Dying!*, suffering chooses Dr. Mark Smith and he responds by allowing God to use it to draw him closer to Christ and to deepen his spiritual walk. This book not only tells an inspirational story of overcoming adversity, but also provides practical applications on how to grow in faith during times of suffering."

—**Dr. Bill Jones**, Chancellor,
Columbia International University

"Do you think that God's supernatural strength given to weak human beings is only something that Bible characters experienced centuries ago, in far-off places? Think again. *Oh God, I'm Dying!* is a modern-day real-life example of two ordinary people, Mark and Debbie Smith, who have seen God do extraordinary things, here and now, in spite of (no, *because of!*) their weakness—and all for His glory."

—**George W. Murray,** Former President & Chancellor, Columbia International University

"Mark's powerful story captures the heart of Columbia International University's message: *To Know Christ and to Make Him Known*. From a life helplessly dependent on God comes compelling faith lessons for the reader. This captivating book is well written and can be life changing for persons experiencing any kind of pain."

—**Delaine Blackwell**, Teaching Director, Community Bible Study, Columbia, SC

OH GOD, I'M DYING!

How God Redeems
Pain for Our Good
and for His Glory

TERRY POWELL & MARK SMITH

NASHVILLE

NEW YORK • LONDON • MELBOURNE • VANCOUVER

OH GOD, I'M DYING!
How God Redeems Pain for Our Good and for His Glory

© 2021 TERRY POWELL & MARK SMITH

Published in New York, New York, by Morgan James Publishing. Morgan James is a trademark of Morgan James, LLC. www.MorganJamesPublishing.com

Scripture taken from the NEW AMERICAN STANDARD BIBLE ®, Copyright © 1960, 1962, 1968, 1971, 1972, 1973, 1975, 1977, 1995 by the Lockman Foundation. Used by permission.

ISBN 978-1-64279-990-3 paperback
ISBN 978-1-64279-991-0 eBook
Library of Congress Control Number: 2020900693

Cover Design by:
Megan Whitney, Creative Ninja Designs
megan@creativeninjadesigns.com

Morgan James is a proud partner of Habitat for Humanity Peninsula and Greater Williamsburg. Partners in building since 2006.

Get involved today! Visit
www.MorganJamesBuilds.com

DEDICATIONS

Mark Smith

Debbie Smith

This book is dedicated to my wife Debbie, who has been the ultimate servant. And to my sons, Douglas and Micah, and Daughter-in-Love, Kierston, who inspire me daily to keep going. Thank you all for enduring the painful days with me!

Terry Powell

Lynn Hoekstra (Lady Rembrandt), College of Education Faculty, CIU

From her teacher's palette, on the canvas of her classroom, she blends primary colors that result in an eye-pleasing masterpiece: content mastery; creative strategies for learner engagement; enthusiastic verbal and nonverbal communication, plus strong application. To God's grace gift of teaching, she adds diligent preparation, technical proficiency and the most important educational principle of all: love for students. Lynn utilizes what she has learned about the *science* of teaching to create priceless *art*.

After she led a workshop for teachers visiting our campus, I left thinking, "*That was a Rembrandt!*" Lynn epitomizes the excellence that marks the faculty at Columbia International University.

Hope Chenault (First Lady of Servanthood) Faculty Administrative Assistant, Seminary and School of Ministry

Hope kept me going by expressing enthusiasm for the story, and complimenting my writing of it. Yet more than once, she suggested revisions that qualified what I had written, pointing out that *how* one person experiences God's grace and intervention isn't necessarily the norm for every believer. She often contributed to the clarity of the writing, explaining how her perception of my meaning did not match my intent. To Hope's wisdom, add an infectious laugh, genuine concern for the faculty with whom she works, a tender heart for hurting people, and a servant heart. She is a prime example of why administrative assistants and other support staff are integral to effectiveness at Columbia International University.

TABLE OF CONTENTS

Should you read this book?
YES ...

If you or a loved one experiences chronic pain, illness, or another form of suffering that won't go away.

If your pain sometimes generates despondency and siphons off your joy.

If, as a Christian, you often struggle to reconcile your pain with a God who is loving, good, and wise.

If you want to see how various means of God's grace sustain a person and his wife through a deep adversity.

If the enemy of your soul tries to convince you that your brokenness disqualifies you from great usefulness to God.

If someone else caused your pain and resentment tries to burrow its way into your heart.

If you've come to the point of exclaiming, "*Oh God, please — don't waste my pain!*"

If you want to see how your faith can deepen and your fruitfulness increase not *in spite of* pain, but *because* of it.

Perhaps you do not know Mark and Debbie Smith, but read the story so you will become better acquainted with their Savior and with His sustaining grace. What Jesus has done for and through them, He can do for and through you.

ACKNOWLEDGMENTS

Completing a book requires significant contributions beyond the labor of the writer and the cooperation of the subject of the story.

From Mark Smith

To Jenny Mowery: You were an angel sent to us, especially for Debbie's sake. Thank you for your love and care. We will always love you.

To Pastor Mac: We could not have made it without you and your care. Your daily reading to me from the Word and watching out for Debbie was the best. We love you.

To Dad and Mom: Thanks for allowing us to live with you for a while, for the many trips, the money and for your love and prayers. We will always love you.

To all other family members: Thank you for loving us!

To Debbie Germany: Thanks for your kind assistance and many hours of support! You are the best.

From Terry Powell

Debbie Smith, Mark's wife, wrote a 15-page document containing her recollections of the accident and its aftermath, from which I gleaned liberally. She also gave a 90-minute interview and replied to numerous questions by email.

Craig Brown, Rob Hartman, Andre Rogers and *Elvin Weinmann* offered valuable input through interviews.

Hope Chenault, Greta Clinton, Maria Cochrane, Dolly Powell, and *Peggy Lee Manoogian* read the manuscript, offered suggestions for clarification, and assisted in copyediting. Hope also typed manuscript revisions and added her technical know-how to meet the style and format requirements of the publisher.

I want to thank members of the Morgan James Publishing group for believing in this book project and assisting with its publication. Special kudos go to *Terry Whalin, Wes Taylor, Margo Toulouse,* and persons on the Author Support team.

Kierston Smith provided several photographs that added to the visual appearance of the book.

Thanks to all of my friends and blog subscribers who interceded for this book project. Your prayers enabled me to persist through a myriad of challenges and details.

Mark and I both assert that the One who deserves the most credit for this story is our Redeemer, Jesus Christ. Mark and I know that any usefulness on our part stems from our Lord's sustaining grace. How grateful we are that our Lord delights in using broken, weak instruments to proclaim His might.

FOREWORD

The Christian experience is so characterized by blessing, the abundant life and victory that often we are slow to correlate the providence of a loving God with any adversity we encounter. However, God allows trials and obstacles in our lives to prepare and to strengthen us for a greater purpose than we could otherwise fulfill.

It is a principle of Christian living that overcoming resistance or obstacles produces stronger disciples. An appropriate analogy is exercising with weights in a fitness center. Pushing, pulling and lifting against the obstacle of weights builds stronger, larger muscles and enhances overall health. Though the exercises cause discomfort, perhaps even pain, the outcome is a positive one. Similarly, when God's plan for us includes resistance in the form of adversity, it strengthens our character and usefulness.

In Romans 5:3–4, the apostle Paul asserts, "We also exult in our tribulations, knowing that tribulation brings about perseverance; and perseverance, proven character, and proven character, hope."

In the pages of this book, Mark Smith's story vividly illustrates this principle. He experienced adversity in the form of a life-altering car accident. Initially, there was no way that he could imagine how God would use this tragedy to strengthen and to prepare him for a much greater purpose.

Although Mark couldn't understand God's purpose for the accident and its aftermath, he prayed for and was granted the grace to trust in God's plan for his life. As one who spent several years in the trenches with him, building one of America's fastest-growing private Christian universities, I saw the painful effects of the accident on him daily. I also witnessed how God turned the adversity of the accident into something that ultimately strengthened and developed a unique, extraordinary leadership capacity within Mark.

It is almost impossible to read this book and not see that when one meets adversity with the proper response, multiplied blessings result. When we respond appropriately to trials, we are able to reflect God's glory to a greater degree, and we become a conduit for escalated blessing to others. This book reveals how the "perseverance, character and hope" Paul refers to materialized in Mark's life and leadership, resulting in a blessing to thousands through the universities he has served with and led.

When we observe an effective leader, one whom God is using to accomplish great things, we rarely see or appreciate the adversity the person has overcome that helped produce the success. Mark's story clearly reveals the link between his pain and his effectiveness.

Everyone has a story. This is my friend Mark Smith's story. I know you will be inspired and encouraged as you read it. You will see that when we put our trust in God, when we cling to Him and the promises of His Word, He will take us through the adversity and optimize it for our good and for His glory.

When you finish this story, you won't be thinking, "What a great leader Mark Smith is!" No, you'll be thinking, "What an awesome God we serve!"

—**Craig Brown**, State Director for Ohio,
Faith and Freedom Coalition

PART 1
THE STORY

God's Grace Is Sufficient for All Your Needs

Chapter 1

"WHATEVER YOU FACE, I WILL BE WITH YOU!"

If only his day would have ended as well as it had begun.

On March 3, 1996, 30-year-old Mark Smith, his wife Debbie and their 11-month-old son, Doug, bundled up for a 65-mile drive from their home in Marion, Indiana to Winchester, a smaller Indiana town. Despite the sun's rays bathing the landscape, a cold breeze stung their cheeks as they walked to their Ford Taurus. Yet the warmth inside them, instilled by three recent positive events, more than compensated for the uncomfortable temperature.

Two months earlier, Mark had launched his new, challenging ministry as an academic administrator at Indiana Wesleyan University. In addition, he and Debbie were reveling in their new role as parents. Finally, Mark was on the cusp of his doctorate, having recently submitted his dissertation to the dissertation committee at West Virginia University. Feeling the immense relief of finishing the writing project, Mark eagerly anticipated serving as a guest speaker later that morning at Randolph Friends Church. Having served five years as a pastor, few things kindled more joy within Mark than preaching the Word of God and meeting new people.

A Grace-Filled Sermon

When Mark stepped behind the pulpit, he spoke on one of his favorite themes and passages. He dissected a heart-massaging text on God's ability and willingness to help weak people: 2 Corinthians 12:9–10.

The apostle Paul had been pleading with the Lord to remove what he called a "thorn in the flesh," some type of impediment that Paul believed hindered his ministry. The Lord refused, citing the value of this limitation in keeping Paul humble. Instead of healing Paul, the Lord assured him of an even greater divine intervention: "My grace is sufficient for you, for power is perfected in weakness."

Then Paul did an about-face. "Most gladly, therefore, I will rather boast about my weaknesses, that the power of Christ may dwell in me. Therefore, I am well content with weaknesses, with insults, with distresses, with persecutions, with difficulties, for Christ's sake; for when I am weak, then I am strong."

With exuberance, Mark explained how God turns the world's value system on its head. Instead of applauding human competence and self-sufficiency, God values neediness, a poverty of spirit that leaves His people no other recourse but to depend on Him. God views our weakness as a spiritual asset, providing an opportunity to showcase His power in and through us.

Church members saw Mark's beaming countenance, heard the intensity of his voice and observed expressive gestures that embellished the message. Throughout the sermon, Mark reiterated his main point: "*God's grace is sufficient for any situation that we face.*" They watched and listened as Mark's heart literally overflowed from his lips.

No one present realized that the first person to receive an opportunity to apply the message would be the messenger himself.

An Unexpected Detour

When the service ended, a couple from the congregation with whom Mark and Debbie were already friends hosted them for lunch. With Tim and Esther Dotson, they enjoyed a satisfying meal and catching up on each other's lives. Debbie and their baby stayed with the Dotsons when Mark left at 1:45 p.m. for an interview with the board of a different church. A United Methodist Church in the area was seeking a regular interim preacher while they searched for a new pastor. Mark relished the possibility of preaching more often.

What Mark couldn't anticipate was the calamity waiting to happen just three miles from the Dotsons' house. The driver of an oncoming car, his attention diverted, veered to the left out of his lane and headed directly for Mark's Taurus.

Wham!!

The collision sounded like a small bomb detonating, followed by the grinding noise of metal scraping against metal. The head-on crash crumpled the left front and driver's side of Mark's Taurus as if it were made of pliable plastic. The other driver's abrupt change of direction didn't give Mark time to brake or to swerve out of the way. With Mark going 45 miles per hour and the other driver traveling at 60 miles per hour, the impact was horrific.

The impact knocked Mark's car a total of 80 feet off the road and into the edge of a cornfield. The impact shoved the dashboard and steering column into Mark, pinning him to the seat. Metal from the left front fender area and driver side door slashed into his left arm and lower left side. Blood spewed from multiple gashes, spilling onto his clothes and pooling on the floorboard.

The blow temporarily rendered Mark unconscious. He awoke moments later, unable to move. Though shock initially mollified the degree of pain he felt, Mark knew his condition was critical. Smoke filling the car made breathing difficult. He saw the blood seeping from his body. *Could rescuers get him out before he bled to death?*

"'For I know the plans that I have for you,' declares the Lord, 'plans for welfare and not for calamity, to give you a future and a hope'" (Jeremiah 29:11).

By instinct, Mark cried out to the Person he served and loved the most: *"Oh God, I'm dying!"*

Mark recalls the thoughts that roiled around in his head. "I knew I was facing eternity," Mark recalls. "I didn't want to die. I had lots of reasons to keep living. Yet while in that helpless, uncertain state, the comforting, sweet presence of the Holy Spirit enveloped me. I heard the Spirit whisper, *'Son, you are Mine!'* I realized that going to be with the Lord would be a blessing, for I knew that my sins had been forgiven and Jesus Christ had bled on the cross to make heaven possible for me.

"Then my mind switched to another train of thought, as I wondered about the condition I'd be in if I survived. Was I facing lifelong disability? Would I be able to work? That's when I heard another inside whisper from the Holy Spirit: *'Whatever you face, I will be with you!'*"

Mark heard the wail of sirens drawing closer and closer to the scene. Then the flash of red and blue lights from emergency

Mark's Taurus after rescuers utilized the "jaws of life" to extract Mark from the car.

vehicles streamed into the car. Moments later, the crunching of metal began as rescuers utilized the "jaws of life" to peel away enough metal to extract him from the car.*

He wasn't sure he had a future on earth, but Mark felt the overwhelming presence of the One who controlled his future.

Who was this college administrator and preacher who lay trapped in a mangled car for 45 minutes? What marker events in his first 30 years brought him to this pivotal point in a rural Indiana cornfield? What evidence of God's grace, which He had preached about so passionately that morning, had he already experienced? Would his past experiences with the Lord help Mark pass the formidable tests that lay ahead?

Rescuers airlifted the other driver to a hospital. He also survived the crash.

Chapter 2

"MARK, WILL YOU GIVE ME YOUR HEART?"

A sick pig. A blown engine in an old Ford Mustang. A niggling discomfort over a tax bill. What do these circumstances have in common? Tracing Mark Smith's story prior to the 1996 auto accident answers the question. In this chapter, you'll see what stitched together these predicaments.

A Legacy of Faith

Privileged to have Christian parents, Mark can't remember a time when church wasn't a vital part of his life. He grew up on a small farm near the town of Galax, in southwestern Virginia. Mark attended a church started by his grandmother and her friends, Haven of Rest Bible Church.

A hinge on which his life turned came in the autumn of his tenth year. As he listened to a visiting speaker during a revival service, the Holy Spirit convicted Mark of his sin and convinced him that Jesus had paid the penalty for those sins on the cross. "I was eager to go forward at the end of the service and give my life to Christ," Mark reflects. "Impatient, I was fidgeting in my pew, wishing he'd finish the message and go ahead and give the altar call."

After he yielded his life to Christ that night, he immediately shared what had happened with a neighbor. Mark's proclivity for personal evangelism blossomed during his adolescence. He had no reticence about sharing his faith and made a lasting impact on the faith of a couple of his good friends.

Several books on the role of prayer and faith, given to him by his father, influenced Mark. Andrew Murray's *With Christ in the School of Prayer*, as well as works by George Bevington and Bob Sheffey, especially aided his spiritual formation. At the time, Mark couldn't envision how the seeds sown by those books would burst through the soil and become distinctive features on the landscape of his future leadership.

An incident in his early teens was a precursor of the bold faith that would characterize Mark's future.

Mark's grandmother asked him to raise a pig each year as a way for him to learn about business and responsibility. One year, his young pig wasn't putting on the typical weight. His dad's pig from the same litter was 75–100 pounds heavier. A pig without a huge appetite is an anomaly! Mark knew the gist of James 5:14–15: "Is anyone among you sick? Let him call for the elders of the church, and let them pray over him, anointing him with oil in the name of the Lord; and the prayer offered in faith will restore the one who is sick." Apparently, the pig suffered from a hernia.

"I knew the particulars of those verses didn't fit my situation," Mark says," but I still felt compelled to apply the promise to my pig's illness. Perhaps I was somewhat naïve, but I knew the Bible tells us to take our anxieties to the Lord and I was definitely worried about my pig. I went to our kitchen, grabbed a bottle of Wesson cooking oil, rubbed some of it on my pig and prayed fervently for God to heal him."

And He did!

"And without faith it is impossible to please Him, for he who comes to God must believe that He is, and that He is a rewarder of those who seek him" (Hebrews 11:6).

The pig's appetite returned. His weight began to climb. Before long, the pig had gained scores of pounds and almost caught up with his dad's pig.

Before any reader assigns what happened to coincidence or thinks what Mark did was impertinent, consider the fact that faith pleases God and He promises to reward it (Hebrews 11:6). It is just like God to honor the uncomplicated faith of a child, especially one He would later call to serve where audacious requests would be integral to his job description.

Being a farm boy, Mark cared for a lot of animals. A few became special pets. God didn't answer every prayer a young Mark offered on behalf of an animal. Nonetheless, this extraordinary intervention with his pig boosted Mark's faith, making it more likely that he would trust God with far greater needs in later years. This divine intervention branded into Mark's consciousness the truth that God is willing and able to respond to the heartfelt pleas of His people.

A Change of Direction

As a high school student, Mark excelled in math and science classes and demonstrated an affinity for anything agricultural. He joined his school's Future Farmers of America club, which won a statewide competition. His faith remained strong and enabled him to resist the typical temptations that trip up many adolescents. Mark planned to be a veterinarian. When he was 18, still in high school, God interrupted his career path.

If you want to make God laugh, tell Him your plans!

During his senior year, while cruising with friends near a Hardee's restaurant, a large truck came whisker-close to smashing into the car in which Mark was a passenger. "The near miss scared me," Mark admits. He realized how close he had come to serious injury or to death. He saw how fragile life is and how quickly it can be snuffed out. Thoughts about eternity and what really mattered vied for his attention the rest of the evening.

When he arrived home late that night, he walked by a table where one of his parents had left an issue of *Missionary Herald* magazine. On the back cover Mark saw a verse where Jesus proclaimed the Great Commission: "Go into all the world and preach the gospel to all creation" (Mark 16:15). He sensed the moving of God's Spirit inside him. He heard the Lord say, *"Mark, will you give Me your heart?"* Since Mark already knew Christ as Savior, he sensed that this was a call to serve the Lord vocationally.

Mark understood that this was a seismic shift in direction. He had envisioned running his own veterinary clinic and making a comfortable living. He knew, however, that he couldn't say "no" to the Holy Spirit's wooing. Prompted to talk it over with God, Mark surrendered to God's revision of the blueprint for his future.

Not long after receiving his call, Mark stood in front of his church to declare publicly his change of plans. After graduating from high school, he attended Surry Community College for basic general education courses, then left for Hobe Sound Bible College in Florida.

A Second Phase of Mark's Ministry Calling

God used the Bible college's president to steer Mark toward a specific field of ministry. "Dr. Robert Whitaker took me under his wing," Mark fondly recalls. "When he realized that I didn't have a particular ministry niche in mind, he challenged me to consider Christian college administration that would culminate with the role of president.

"When I prayed about his challenge, the Lord spoke to me and said, 'You were thinking of being a vet, involving four years of college, then four more graduate years required for veterinary practice. Why not give those eight years to study the issues and skills needed to be a college administrator?'"

Dr. Whitaker informed Mark that few Bible college presidents had the academic training needed to excel in a rapidly changing field of Christian higher education. "Most Bible college presidents are former pastors who never took courses related to a president's responsibilities," he explained to Mark. His words resonated with Mark and drove him to his knees to get the Lord's take on this challenge. God's Spirit convinced Mark that this was phase two of his ministry calling. From that day on, he never wavered from the goal of working in a Christian college.

"I will instruct you and teach you in the way which you should go; I will counsel you with my eye upon you" (Psalm 32:8).

Only 20 years old at the time, Mark nonetheless understood that accreditation would require increasingly higher standards for Christian colleges in the future. Intuitively, he realized that maintaining a strong enrollment would necessitate recruitment of highly qualified faculty, marketing know-how, aggressive fundraising and prudent financial management.

In addition to a crystal-clear call to Christian college administration, God gifted Mark with a wife who also attended Hobe Sound Bible College. He was drawn not only to Debbie's beauty, but to her sweet disposition and heart for the Lord. She wanted to be the wife of a minister and Mark had been called to a particular form of ministry. Extremely compatible in both family background and a heart for serving the Lord, they married the summer before his junior year.

After Bible college, Mark's graduate education revealed his resolve to serve in the educational sphere. In 1990, he earned a Master's degree in "College Teaching." He chose "Higher Education Administration" for his doctorate. Before the accident, he completed all the courses for a doctorate, leaving only the defense of his dissertation. Even the topic of his doctoral dissertation disclosed his laser-beam focus on the career goal God had given him: "The Role of the Christian College President."

Yet years before submitting his dissertation, while still in Bible college, the Lord providentially mapped out faith-developing experiences for Mark and Debbie that would prove more formative than any of his courses or degree programs.

The first educational experience in the Lord's specialized curriculum for the Smiths came while they were on a break from Bible college to visit their parents in Virginia and Pennsylvania.

A Blown Engine

Mark and Debbie were traveling in the mountains of West Virginia, two hours from Mark's home in Virginia, returning from a trip to Pennsylvania where they had visited her parents. Their Mustang started sputtering, leaking oil and belching smoke. They barely made it to a gas station. After giving the engine time to cool down, they repeatedly tried to start it, to no avail.

"We prayed together for God to touch our car," Debbie recalls. "We actually laid our hands on the hood as we prayed,"

Mark adds. The next time they put the key in the ignition and turned it, the engine revved up.

As soon as they arrived home they gave the Mustang to Mark's uncle, a mechanic. After hearing their story and inspecting the engine, he looked bewildered. "How did you get this car here?" he asked. "It looks like a rod is broken. You have a blown engine. There's no way this car should have started back at that gas station."

Mark's only comeback was, "It's a God thing!"

Mark and Debbie acknowledge that the Lord doesn't rescue every believer who is stranded on the highway. Once again, He intervened in an extraordinary way that would sear the event into Mark's memory bank, ultimately inspiring him to ask God for even bigger things in future leadership roles.

A Looming Tax Deadline

In the spring of Mark's senior year, shortly before Bible college graduation, Mark and Debbie faced a financial dilemma. They were learning experientially that God's exams on the matter of faith don't come in the form of essay questions, true/false statements or multiple-choice alternatives.

A month ahead of the tax filing deadline, they discovered they would owe $278. For a couple in school living on a shoestring budget, that was a whopping amount. Extra work was not available as a means of coming up with the money. Their only recourse was to go to Someone who did have the means. For 30 days, they committed to fast from certain meals and to pray fervently each day for the money. They agreed to tell no one of their need, not even relatives.

According to Mark, "We claimed Philippians 4:19 as a promise that applied to our situation: 'My God shall supply all your needs according to His riches in glory in Christ Jesus.' Paul wrote this promise to a church that had been giving sacrificially to his own ministry. Our finances were tight because we had followed God's guidance to attend Bible college. God certainly didn't owe us anything, but we believed He would meet the needs that resulted from our obedience."

"Faithful is He who calls you, and He also will bring it to pass" (1 Thessalonians 5:24).

Before the 30 days expired, the youth group back in Mark's home church took up a collection and mailed $153 to him. His grandmother felt the nudge of God's Spirit to send Mark and Debbie $100. Before she wrote the check, she told her husband what she planned to do. He told her, "Add another $25 from me!"

To the penny, they received $278 to pay the tax bill on time! "We didn't feel that *we* had passed a test so much as *the Lord* had," Mark insists. "He had proved Himself again. What He did strengthened our faith and glorified His name."

A Pastoral Tenure

After earning his Master's degree, Mark honed the management skills he would later need in a school setting by working as a hospital administrator in Terra Alta, West

Virginia. During the same five-year period (1991-1995), he launched his doctoral studies at West Virginia University and pastored a Wesleyan church in Terra Alta. Mark believed that fulfilling God's call to be a Christian college president required hands-on experience in a ministry venue where a majority of the graduates would serve.

When he arrived at the church, average attendance was less than 30. Mark's passionate preaching and shepherding of the members wooed more people to the congregation. When he left the position five years later, average attendance hovered around 110.

Mark had heard that as far back as 17 years earlier, members had occasionally broached the need for a new sanctuary to replace the deteriorating one. However, until Mark arrived, the talk never morphed into action. Believing they needed the facility and convinced God could supply the funds, their 25-year-old new pastor rallied the people, declaring, "Let's do it!" With steadily rising attendance and members captivated by Mark's visionary attitude, they constructed a $350,000 facility that they paid off by the time Mark left Terra Alta.

"I didn't want to leave a congregation saddled with debt," Mark explains. "I firmly believe that you should pay for what you envision."

Four things had happened to deepen Mark's faith: the healing of his pig, the miraculous rejuvenation of a blown engine, the provision for his tax bill and the $350,000 dollars raised in a small church in a short period of time. The car wreck on March 3, 1996 would pose, by far, his most difficult challenge to date.

Trapped in a battered Taurus, in critical condition, overwhelmed with uncertainty about his future, how would Mark respond to the devastating injuries caused by the crash? How could such a catastrophic event fit into what had been a history of God's extraordinary favor toward Mark?

Chapter 3

"HONEY, I'M HERE!"

Before illustrating highlights of Mark Smith's faith development in Chapter 2 and identifying marker events prior to the accident, we left him trapped in his car in critical condition, waiting for rescue. Debbie and their baby were with Tim and Esther Dotson, who had hosted the Smiths for lunch.

The accident occurred on March 3, 1996.

When people congregated around Mark's crumpled Taurus, the only thing he had the strength to say to them was Tim Dotson's phone number. When Tim answered the phone, Debbie noticed that he didn't speak for a couple minutes and saw the grim look on his face.

Before Tim hung up the phone, Debbie blurted, "It's about Mark!"

After Tim confirmed her worst fears, Debbie admits, "From that moment on, everything seemed like a blur. All that mattered was getting to Mark. As Tim drove us to the scene, though I silently prayed the whole time, I was worried sick."

When she spotted Mark's car from a distance, a crack zigzagged across Debbie's heart. "I didn't see how anyone could survive a crash that bad," she thought. When Tim edged closer to the car, his own heart lurched when he saw a blanket draped over Mark's body. He thought it meant Mark had died, but a thoughtful bystander had merely covered him to stave off the cold.

As a helicopter airlifted the other driver to a hospital, rescuers ripped apart Mark's Taurus in order to open up a space large enough to get him out. Debbie remembers thinking, "I can replace the car, but I can't replace my husband or the father of my baby." As she edged closer, she saw Mark's right hand gripping the steering wheel. "That gave me hope that he had some strength left."

When they put Mark on a stretcher, she ran up to him and cried aloud, "Honey, I'm here!" Though he couldn't respond to her at the time, Mark heard her, later acknowledging how precious her words sounded to him at that moment.

In the emergency room, before they started Mark on a series of tests to determine the extent of his injuries, she again made it to his side. Blood stained his shredded clothes and mottled his forehead and cheeks, a result of cuts caused by the shattering of the windshield. "I wanted to burst into tears," Debbie admits, "but I kept them in for Mark's sake."

"When I am afraid, I will put my trust in Thee. In God, whose word I praise, in God I have put my trust; I shall not be afraid. What can mere man to do me?" (Psalm 56:3-4)

Debbie knew Mark had lost a lot of blood. She noticed that he couldn't move. His energy was flagging. What she didn't yet know was the extent to which the impact had pulverized his body.

An Ominous Outlook

The surgeon on duty, Dr. Greg Hellwarth, reported the test results to Mark and Debbie. Two findings comprised the good news: no serious head injuries and no internal bleeding. That increased the likelihood of Mark's survival, but his condition was still critical due to extensive blood loss and the surgeries he faced.

The bad news involved his hip and left arm. Instead of fracturing his hip, the impact had crushed it into multiple pieces, "some so small that if I held them in my hand, they could sift through my fingers like sand," the doctor reported.

Dr. Hellwarth expressed urgency about the arm, indicating surgery on it was a priority over the hip. He described a long and risky operation. "I'm not sure we can save it," he admitted, citing multiple fractures on the forearm and catastrophic damage to the elbow.

When Mark had first met Dr. Hellwarth, before the tests, he looked up and said, "Doctor, will you help me?"

Later the surgeon referred to the kind, gentle way in which Mark had asked for his help. Mark's attitude made Dr. Hellwarth conclude that Mark was a Christian. Though the surgeon had just completed a multi-hour surgery, he was moved when he saw Mark and asked the Lord for extra assistance for yet another surgery.

A devout Christian himself, the surgeon knew it would take his surgical team's best effort—and more—to save Mark's arm. Dr. Hellwarth gathered the other four members of the surgical team around Mark's bed and prayed for him. They asked the Lord for discernment in decision-making and for Him to guide their hands. They rolled Mark into surgery in the late afternoon and didn't finish until 2:00 a.m.

The team saved Mark's arm, but it wouldn't ever be completely whole again.

They implanted bone stimulators in his forearm to support and to accelerate recovery. That involved fastening electrodes in the fractured area, connecting them to tiny battery packs that generated impulses. The purpose was to stimulate bone-forming cells and to mineralize new bone. Mark lost almost three inches of bone in the arm. The surgeon inserted the electrodes and battery packs under the skin.

Mark also left the operating room with a cumbersome-looking visible aid to expedite bone growth: an external fixator over his elbow. This involved drilling holes on either side of the fracture, putting pins and screws into the holes and attaching them to clamps and rods outside of the skin. The goal was to prevent arm movement that would hinder healing and bone formation.

Though grateful they didn't amputate his arm, 24 years later, Mark's left arm has less muscle mass and strength than his right arm. Rub your finger across his elbow and you can feel the head of a screw they inserted.

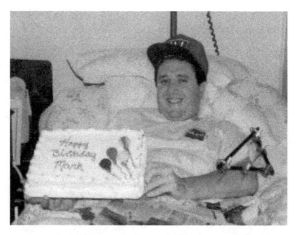

A fixator restricted Mark's arm movement
so the implanted bone stimulators could
mineralize new bone near his elbow.

Excruciating Pain

Because of the trauma his body had experienced on Sunday, his physician didn't think Mark had the strength to tolerate another major surgery until Friday. That meant Mark lay on his crushed hip for five days and nights. Despite the IV that dripped morphine into his body, moving even an inch resulted in screams prompted by a volcanic eruption of pain. More than once, the pain rifled through him so suddenly that he passed out. They also treated him for stomach ulcers caused by the stretching of the lining of his stomach upon impact. A cut in his sciatic nerve exacerbated his pain.

Seeing how little the medicine assuaged Mark's pain weighed heavily on Debbie. "Once they came to get him for an X-ray," she recalls. "He hollered from the pain and I had to turn my head away. When someone you love hurts that much, it makes you hurt as well."

"Behold, God is my helper; the Lord is the sustainer of my soul" (Psalm 54:4).

Before the hip surgery, Dr. Hellwarth gave them more grim news. "The outcome is uncertain," he noted. "There's a possibility Mark will never walk again, or if he does, it will be with great difficulty."

After surgery he still couldn't assure them of a positive outcome. In an effort to repair the hip, he had inserted thirteen screws to reconnect pieces of the bone. "He's facing months of painful physical therapy to learn to walk again," Dr. Hellwarth explained, "and right now I can't guarantee how well he will recover."

The horrific pain, the inability to sleep more than an hour or two at a time and the looming uncertainty about his recovery resulted in a strenuous first week for Mark and Debbie.

How could Debbie cope with caring for Mark and for their 11-month-old son? The hospital's distance from their home amounted to an hour-and-a-half round trip of driving, figuring just one trip each day.

If he were disabled, how would Mark fulfill what he perceived was a God-given calling to be a Christian college president? The administrative role he had recently accepted and the eventual office of president would require lots of energy and travel representing the school.

How would the Lord meet their physical, emotional and financial needs during the difficult months ahead? How would He demonstrate the truth of His all-sufficient grace which Mark had emphasized in his sermon shortly before the accident?

Chapter 4

"LORD, WILL YOU
DO THIS FOR ME?"

Debbie's Dilemma

Mark lies flat on his back, his days bookended with severe pain. You live a 45-minute one-way drive from the hospital. He needs your physical presence as well as your emotional support, due to the uncertainty about his long-term recovery.

You yearn to be with him around the clock, but caring for your 11-month-old son makes that impossible. Your anguish escalates when, while Mark is still hospitalized, your out-of-state mother falls seriously ill and goes to the hospital—and you cannot go to her side.

How do you manage your own need for bodily rest and stability of spirit? How do you cope with the competing demands on your time and energy? You feel like soft taffy pulled in different directions by the pressing needs of the people you love most. What sources can you tap into for the strength to take the next step, to fulfill the next responsibility? How will the Lord lavish His grace on you?

Mark's Crisis

You didn't know that a human being could hurt so much and survive. If it weren't for the high dosage of morphine, you can't imagine how grievous the pain would be.

The physical ache isn't your only tormentor. The medicine prevents sound sleep. All you can get is anywhere from a few minutes to an hour at a time, and even then nightmares plague you. You are back in the mangled Taurus, in shock, unable to move, choking on smoke that is filling up the car. The weariness leaves your mind engulfed in a fog, hindering concentration when someone visits you.

The bleak prognosis about your physical recovery perturbs you. Will you ever work full time again? If so, when? How will you pay the bills that are piling up? You know your insurance won't pay all the costs.

Worse yet, when you wake up during the night, loneliness overwhelms you and there's no one by your side. You send Debbie home late each afternoon so she doesn't drive after dark.

That leaves you with a long stretch of time without a physical presence to stifle your fears and to buoy your spirits.

One night, you are so discouraged that tears cascade down your cheeks. Though it's 2:00 a.m., you call Debbie. You desperately need to share your despondency with her, to hear your beloved's voice and her reassurances.

You are an optimistic, energetic, visionary leader. How do you—a driven, Type A personality—deal with a state of total helplessness? How will the robust faith in God for which you are known withstand this crisis? How will God's Spirit come alongside and sustain you?

Grace in Person

They had been living in Marion, Indiana only three months. They had not yet settled on a home church, though they had attended a church pastored by a longtime friend, Rev. Mac McCrary. You wouldn't know they were new to the area by the extraordinary ministrations of God's people.

That Sunday afternoon, unfolding all the way into Monday morning when they finished Mark's surgery at 2:00 a.m., there was always at least one person alongside Debbie. The poor health of her parents made their coming unworkable. Mark's parents, sister and brother-in-law would not arrive until Monday evening from Virginia. New friends, as well as old ones, compensated for the absence of immediate family during those crucial first couple of days.

Jenny Mowery, a long-time friend of Debbie, drove an hour and a half to join her at Ball Memorial Hospital. The church leaders with whom Mark was planning to meet sent out an email for urgent prayer on Mark's behalf. A couple of Mark's colleagues at Indiana Wesleyan University saw the email and rushed to the hospital.

Rev. Mac McCrary, whose church they had visited, drove a half hour and stayed with Debbie until Mark was in the recovery room, in serious but stable condition. Then Mrs. McCrary took Debbie to her home for a few hours of sleep. Mark and Debbie had known Pastor McCrary and his wife since their college days, when they were classmates of the McCrarys' children. Another pastor they had met, Dan Keaton, also supported Debbie during this crisis.

In addition to the help of Tim and Esther Dotson, who had kept their son Doug for the day, Jenny became a mainstay among the volunteers who helped take care of Doug and household chores. The help of these three friends, as well as others, freed Debbie to visit Mark each day. After Mark's family left, Jenny stayed in the Smiths' home a day or two each week when Mark was in the hospital.

"Bear one another's burdens, and thus fulfill the law of Christ" (Galatians 6:2).

When Mark's family did arrive, his dad, John Smith, offered vital assistance to Debbie. He advised her on insurance matters and helped her find a replacement car. Mark's sister, Susan, and her husband, also named Mark, had driven Mark's mom and dad to Ohio. Along with Mark's parents, they assisted in a multitude of ways.

Debbie reflects on their week-long visit: "You never know how important family is until a tragedy occurs. Mark's dad was like a rock to me and his mom was a prayer warrior. We counted so much on those prayers. The presence of his family made a huge difference."

The phone also became a conduit through which others' love for them flowed. "When I'd get home each evening from the hospital," Debbie reflects, "a highlight of my day was listening to the many phone messages left by people, assuring us of their prayers and concern."

A few members of the church Mark had pastored in West Virginia put rubber to their prayers, driving to Ohio and visiting Mark in the hospital and assisting Debbie. Within the first few weeks after the accident, Mark and Debbie received at least 400 cards and notes. Though no one had solicited funds, many of the cards included money. Within several months they received over $10,000 to help pay the medical bills.

"I'm the type of person who wants to handle things myself," Debbie acknowledges. "I hesitate to make my needs known. But after the accident, I didn't have a choice but to rely on others and to accept, with gratitude, their offers to help. So many people were interceding for us that I literally, physically, felt the effect of the prayers."

Rev. Mac McCrary made daily, unhurried visits to the hospital. He sidled up to Mark's bed, prayed fervently for him and read Bible passages aloud to soothe his spirit. Mark could not physically pick up a Bible and read it for himself.

Pastor McCrary's church gave a love offering to help the Smiths. Despite Mark's frail condition, he kept urging Mark to keep his eye on God's calling on his life, instilling hope within Mark that his ministry was not permanently derailed. "He is my encourager to this day, 24 years later," Mark said recently.

Throughout the long months of Mark's recovery, members of the body of Christ kept serving the Smiths through prayers, meals, babysitting, financial gifts and their presence. Mark and Debbie experienced the truth of Proverbs 17:17: "A friend loves at all times, and a brother is born for adversity."

A different means of grace also proved integral to Mark and Debbie's spiritual equilibrium during this crisis.

Grace in Print

A special means of sustaining grace for Mark and Debbie was the Bible that they had long loved, taught, and to some extent, had memorized. Their meditation on God's promises and attributes helped to shift their focus away from the pain and bleak outlook onto the One who loved them and controlled their circumstances.

You have already read how Mark couldn't pick up a Bible for a long time after the accident. That is when God's Sprit reminded Mark of pertinent passages he had memorized, such as Romans 8:28: "We know that God causes all things to work together for good to those who love God, to those who are called according to His purpose."

Mark says, "I knew I loved God and that He had called me to salvation as well as to a ministry in Christian college administration. Though at the time I couldn't see a *why* for the accident, this verse reminded me that God controls my circumstances and He could design a positive outcome despite the bleak outlook."

When Mark's emotions would rise and fall like sea waves, Luke 1:37 anchored his spirit: "Nothing will be impossible with God."

An angel had informed Mary that she would bear the Son of God. Mary wondered how she could conceive a son without having relations with a man. Mark believed that the angel's words to her also pertained to him, especially when physicians questioned whether he would ever walk again or recover enough physically to manage a demanding full-time ministry. The verse kept reminding Mark of God's capability and took the spotlight off his own weakened condition.

Philippians 4:13 also fueled Mark's faith during the difficult months of recovery: "I can do all things through Him who strengthens me." In the preceding verses (11–12), Paul explained that he had learned to be content in all types of circumstances. What enabled Paul to endure and to stay fruitful during difficulty was the strength Christ provided.

Mark insists, "The key to this verse is not the words 'I can do.' Rather, the words that deserve highlighting are 'through Him.' My pain and neediness convinced me, like never before, that if God ever accomplished anything else in my life, it would be 'through Him who strengthens me.' When you are as weak and as fragile as I was after the accident, you discover that there is no other source of strength but Him."

The text most precious to Mark during his recovery was Psalm 34, especially verses 1–7.

> *I will bless the Lord at all times;*
> *His praise shall continually be in my mouth.*
> *My soul shall make its boast in the Lord;*
> *the humble shall hear it and rejoice.*
> *O magnify the Lord with me,*
> *and let us exalt His name together.*
> *I sought the Lord and He answered me,*
> *and delivered me from all my fears.*
> *They looked to Him and were radiant,*
> *and their faces shall never be ashamed.*
> *This poor man cried and the Lord heard him,*
> *and saved him out of all his troubles.*
> *The angel of the Lord encamps around those who fear Him,*
> *and rescues them.*

Through these words, God's Spirit inspired Mark to praise the Lord no matter how he felt (vs.1–2). God's glory and renown, rather than his own reputation, became Mark's consuming passion (vs.3). The Psalmist's experience of seeking the Lord as a way to relieve his fears prompted Mark to vent all his apprehensions to the Lord (vs.4).

Mark asked the Lord to renew within him a radiant, positive spirit for which he was known prior to the accident, rather than allowing him to descend into self-pity or negativism (vs.5). Mark felt weak and needy, or "poor" as the text says, and knew that his only hope was the Lord's enablement (vs.6).

"This is my comfort in my affliction, that Thy Word has revived me" (Psalm 119:50).

The Holy Spirit also stabilized and instilled hope within Debbie through the Word He had inspired.

"Psalm 121 is my favorite passage," Debbie exclaims. "I consulted it over and over during the hard weeks after Mark's wreck." The first two verses kept her mind's trajectory on the Lord, rather than mired in the uncertainty of Mark's condition: "I will lift up my eyes to the mountains; from whence shall my help come? My help comes from the Lord, who made heaven and earth."

When she was getting less-than-needed sleep due to her treks back and forth to the hospital, plus caring for her son, the next two verses in Psalm 121 were especially meaningful to her. "He will not allow your foot to slip; He who keeps you will not slumber. Behold, He who keeps Israel will neither slumber nor sleep." Debbie rejoiced in His round-the-clock care. Other meaningful parts of the chapter included, "The Lord is your keeper" (vs.5) and "He will keep your soul" (vs.7). Mark's accident had rattled her soul, but God's Word kept it in alignment.

Isaiah 30:15, in tandem with Psalm 91, were other texts that massaged Debbie's heart. The Lord is the speaker in the verse from Isaiah: "In repentance and rest you shall be saved, in quietness and trust is your strength." The late pastor Ron Dunn once said, "No one trusts the Lord until he *has* to!"[1] Debbie was enmeshed in a *have-to* situation and the trust fueled by God's Word quieted her soul.

From Psalm 91, descriptions of the Lord reminded Debbie that she had a secure place to go with her fears and needs. In this single chapter, words depicting our God include refuge, fortress, shield, bulwark and dwelling place. She feasted on the promise that capped this chapter, given to the person who trusts the Lord: "He will call upon Me, and I will answer him; I will be with him in trouble; I will rescue him, and honor him. With a long life I will satisfy him, and let him behold My salvation" (Psalm 91:15–16).

The texts cited represent many other parts of Scripture that comforted Mark and Debbie. Both mentioned verses in which God pledges to hear the cry of His people. Those promises construct a bridge that leads us to the next means of grace they latched onto.

Grace Through Prayer

Delving into God's Word typically compels us to pray. For example, some texts expose sin, then the Holy Spirit's conviction generates confession. Or, as with the texts that consoled Mark and Debbie, verses pulsate with promises that motivate us to cry out to Him for their fulfillment in our stressful situation.

In Psalm 62, David's depictions of God first nourished Debbie's soul. David described Him as a rock, stronghold, our salvation and refuge. Then verse 8 provided her with an incentive to approach His throne daily on behalf of Mark: "Trust in Him at all times, O people; pour out your heart before Him. God is a refuge for us."

"So often I felt physically exhausted and emotionally drained," Debbie remembers. "I had nowhere else to go but to Him. I poured out my heart to Him so many times that I don't see how He could keep from growing weary of me. I know, though, that He never got tired of my pleading, because His Word so often invites us to come to Him with our needs."

God's Word prompted confession from Debbie as well as petition. "A few times I felt bitterness creeping in, because all that Mark was going through wasn't his fault. In my head, I knew God was in control and that He could redeem Mark's plight for our good and for His own glory. But it took a while for my heart to catch up with what I knew about God," Debbie explains.

"I'd see Mark so discouraged he'd cry or I'd watch him yell from pain during physical therapy, when he was just trying to take a step, and I'd start feeling anger and frustration. Then the Spirit would convict me and I'd cry out to Him for forgiveness, seeking His power to release any resentment."

Debbie's prayers of confession cracked the crust of resentment forming over her heart. What her head believed about God's control and goodness started seeping into her heart, changing her attitude.

Heartfelt prayers undergirded Mark as well. Mark learned early in life to rely on prayer and faith. God's repeated interventions had planted within him an ever-increasing capacity to trust Him.

Those needs previously met by the Lord paled in comparison to the stark helplessness of Mark's condition the week after the accident. The combination of pain, limited sleep, nightmares and discouragement resulted in a new crescendo of impassioned pleas to God from his hospital bed.

"And call upon Me in the day of trouble; I shall rescue you, and you will honor Me" (Psalm 50:15).

Mark's most vivid recollection of answered prayer occurred the sixth night after the accident. Doctors had expressed concern over regression in Mark's vital signs. They indicated that he could face up to six months in the hospital and nine months of physical therapy. Though this deflated Mark's spirit, what preoccupied him was a desperate need for rest.

That is when he made his appeal: "Lord, I'm so tired of this. Lord, will you please take away the nightmares? I want to sleep better tonight. Lord, will You do this for me?" According to Mark, he immediately fell asleep after quoting Psalm 34:7: "The angel of the Lord encamps around those who fear Him, and rescues them."

That evening Mark slept for over four consecutive hours, easily the longest uninterrupted span since the accident. No nightmares badgered him.

The Lord's gracious response to Mark's plea included not only peaceful sleep, but what Mark calls "the undeniable, sweet presence of the Lord" after he awoke. "I know the Lord is always with His people," Mark explains, "but what I experienced in the early hours of that morning was an extraordinary consciousness of His presence, resulting in extreme serenity of spirit.

"I looked toward the foot of my bed and saw a childlike figure. This was not anyone I knew, nor a hospital staff member. The figure appeared to be praying for me. The figure never spoke to me, didn't stay in the room long and never reappeared during my hospital stay.

"I know I have to tread carefully here," Mark concedes, "when it comes to interpreting this experience. I cannot say this emphatically, but I believe God sent a ministering angel to me just when I needed comfort the most."

Mark bases his viewpoint of this visitor on Psalm 34:7, which he mentally reviewed right before falling asleep, and on Psalm 91:11–12: "He will give His angels charge concerning you, to guard you in all your ways. They will bear you up in their hands."

Mark puts an exclamation point on this experience. "What I *can* say for sure is that the Lord gave me an unparalleled awareness of His presence and concern that morning! But I do believe that He sent His angel."

When Pastor McCrary visited Mark a few hours later, what he sensed and said—before Mark had spoken—confirmed that something extraordinary had occurred in the room. As soon as he entered Mark's room, the spiritually sensitive pastor seemed taken aback.

"What is going on in here?" he inquired. "This room is bright like the hue of the presence of God." He, too, felt the unusually strong presence of the Lord. Before he left that morning, Pastor McCrary added, "God will show you that something special happened in this room."

The body of Christ.

The Word of God.

Heartfelt prayer.

These means of grace would continue to sustain Mark and Debbie long after his release from the hospital, which transpired much quicker than physicians had anticipated—just 21 days after the accident.

Yet on the long road to recovery that Mark and Debbie were traveling, potholes and steep hills still awaited them. When Mark arrived home, confined to a hospital bed, Debbie no longer had hospital staff to assist with Mark's care. When that realization dawned, she cried, "Oh God, I'm on my own. I need help!"

When physicians started weaning Mark off powerful pain meds, he experienced a new type of misery that rivaled the physical pain. When a follow-up visit to his surgeon brought bad news, Mark's mood plummeted to its lowest level ever.

Chapter 5 unveils the reality that God's people experience ups as well as downs, both circumstantially and emotionally. It also illustrates that for every color of trial, there is a corresponding color of God's grace.

Chapter 5

"OH GOD, I CAN'T
DO THIS ANYMORE!"

Mark's release from Ball Memorial Hospital after only 21 days defied physicians' initial expectations. They had mentioned the possibility of a stay extending as long as six months. What a joy to get out of the sterile medical environment and to enter the warm atmosphere of home!

Though he was still confined to a hospital bed and faced painful, five-day-a-week physical therapy sessions, coming home boosted Mark's spirits. The best part was seeing the excitement of his one-year-old son at having his dad nearby. Doug sat next to Mark's bed, exuberantly jabbering, apparently catching his dad up on all that happened over the previous three weeks.

Yet the adversity was not over for Mark and Debbie, not by a long shot.

Now that nurses weren't nearby around the clock, Debbie's ministrations to and responsibility for Mark would increase exponentially. Being weaned off strong painkillers in the weeks ahead would afflict Mark in a way he never imagined. And Mark didn't yet know that his time inside a hospital room was not over.

This chapter elaborates on these additional tests to the Smiths' faith.

Depending on Debbie

"Mark required lots of TLC!" Debbie states. "If I could feed, bathe and dress Mark and Doug by noon, I felt like I had accomplished a lot. Giving Mark a wipe-off bath as he lay in bed wasn't easy due to all the maneuvering, while trying to minimize his pain. Caring for him involved lots of mundane tasks, but I considered them a blessing, not drudgery, because I had come so close to losing him."

Debbie describes one incident that almost generated a 911 call.

"Mark said he was tired of getting wipe-off baths in bed, so he was determined to get into the tub. Getting him in it was hard enough, but getting him out of the bathtub was almost impossible. I could just imagine what the 911 operator would say when I told him or her that I needed help because my husband was stuck in the tub! But we kept trying, me straining to heft him up and Mark helping by using his right arm and leg to brace himself. It took a while and Mark winced in pain, but we did it!"

Concerning Debbie's care for Mark at home, one of her friends said, "I don't know how you do it. I don't think I could do all that!" Debbie admits to being afraid at first of caring for Mark all alone. In addition to the physical care, Debbie took over responsibilities that had been Mark's domain, such as paying bills and handling other family business.

She kept crying out to God for the patience and energy needed. She determined that there were too many things to do to waste time asking, "Why did this happen?," or stewing over negative thoughts such as, "All this is so unfair!" God gave her the grace to keep putting one foot in front of the other and asking herself, "Now what needs to be done next?"

Chapter 4 illustrated Debbie's and Mark's reliance on the help of others, the comfort of God's Word and heartfelt prayer. Debbie cites a fourth avenue of grace that sustained her, both before and after Mark arrived home.

Listening to Lyrics

"Some days I was so tired and emotionally numb, I couldn't concentrate enough to read the Bible as was my custom. Even then, I found a way to receive help from Scripture. The Christian music tapes I regularly played often consisted of biblical texts put to music, so the Holy Spirit employed that means to fuel my soul with His Word." After he arrived home, Debbie and Mark often watched Gaither Homecoming videos produced by Bill and Gloria Gaither.

The lyrics of time-tested hymns offered hope and nourished their faith.

"Serve the Lord with gladness; come before Him with joyful singing" (Psalm 100:2).

Music was also an avenue of grace for Mark. When his spirit sagged, God's Spirit used hymns to massage his mind and restore his focus on the gospel. A special hymn for him during his recovery was "My Faith Has Found a Resting Place," written in the 19th century by Eliza Hewitt. His current condition wasn't restful, but Mark found a resting place at the cross. The first and fourth stanzas were especially meaningful to him:

My faith has found a resting place,
Not in device or creed;
I trust the Ever-Living One,
His wounds for me shall plead.
My Great Physician heals the sick,
The lost He came to save;
For me His precious blood He shed,
For me His life He gave.

The music that calmed their souls was especially needed in light of the inner turmoil Mark still experienced.

Releasing the Resentment

Whenever Mark looked back and thought about the accident, it fomented a negative attitude and a tinge of

SALVATION BY GRACE

436   **My Faith Has Found a Resting Place**

Lidie H. Edwards, 1891
Alt. 1990

LANDAS C.M.ref.
André Grétry, 1741–1833
Arr. William J. Kirkpatrick, 1891

resentment. Clearly, the other driver's mistake caused the Smiths a lot of short and long-term pain. When he sensed bitterness welling up, Mark immediately asked the Lord to uproot it and to instill within him a positive mindset. "I rolled it over to God," Mark remembers. "I said to Him, 'God, in Your strength, I forgive him.'"

An out-of-the-ordinary decision the Smiths made also expedited his forgiveness of the driver. "A lawyer told me that winning a two-million-dollar lawsuit was a cinch," Mark recalls. Their medical bills far exceeded their insurance coverage, so it seemed prudent to file a lawsuit.

"Debbie and I prayed about the lawsuit," Mark explains, "but God's Spirit didn't give us the freedom to proceed." (Later, they discovered that the other driver's limited assets would have dramatically altered the amount of money they would have actually received.)

"Let all bitterness and wrath and anger and clamor and slander be put away from you, along with all malice. And be kind to one another, tender-hearted, forgiving each other, just as God in Christ also has forgiven you" (Ephesians 4:31-32).

Based on his experience with severely injured patients, Mark's surgeon offered a medical perspective that buttressed their decision not to sue. Dr. Hellwarth said, "You are one of the few accident victims I've known who didn't sue the person at fault. If you had pursued a long and protracted lawsuit, you would have kept rehashing the accident and your mind would have dwelt on the injustice of all you've been through. I'm convinced that your body is healing faster than expected because you did *not* sue, because your focus is on the future and getting better. If you had put time and energy into a lawsuit," explained the physician, "I believe the likelihood of bitterness would have been far greater."

In retrospect, a decision that seemed foolish to some eventually mirrored the wisdom of God's guidance.

Descending into Depression

Periods of discouragement pockmarked Mark's initial stay in the hospital. Gut-wrenching pain, total dependence on others for the body's needs, acute loneliness at night and a pessimistic prognosis would negatively affect the mood of any human being, even one as enthusiastic and optimistic as Mark.

The time he phoned Debbie at 2:00 a.m., weeping and yearning to hear her voice, was a case in point.

But there's a world of difference between moments of discouragement and full-blown depression.

He had been on morphine for 17 days in the hospital, then doctors switched him to Percocet and Lortab. A week or two after he came home they started taking him off the meds. What he didn't expect was the horrific impact of withdrawal.

Multiple research studies have exposed a strong correlation between going off painkillers and the onset of depression. The meds decrease pain by binding to brain receptors, lowering their capacity to perceive pain. These drugs also reset brain chemistry, making it harder for patients to experience pleasure once they are no longer receiving the medicine.

Mark fell from the chemical highs of the meds to a rock-bottom level of despondency he had never experienced. He bluntly describes a several-week period as "hell on earth." It was as if dark, low-lying clouds rolled in and covered his spirit, blocking all rays of the sun. Hopelessness replaced his usual zest for life. "There were moments when I wasn't coherent or thinking right," he admits. "I couldn't see any purpose for living. I felt so low I could have taken my own life."

"Why are you in despair, O my soul? And why have you become disturbed within me? Hope in God, for I shall yet praise Him, the help of my countenance, and my God" (Psalm 42:11).

Perhaps the lowest point came during a follow-up visit with his surgeon, who gave him disconcerting news. "Your left arm isn't healing properly. You need another surgery." That would mean an additional week in the hospital. This news, coming at a time when he was already affected by the drug withdrawal, resulted in an even worse nosedive in mood.

On the way home from the doctor's appointment, Mark began crying. He said to Debbie, who was driving, "I can't face another surgery!" Then he asked her to pull off the highway and stop. Through his tears, he began spilling his frustration in a prayer that started with these words: "*Oh God, I can't do this anymore!*"

Ironically, Mark was modeling the biblical concept of lament, taking our pain to the Lord and expressing our raw emotions. Faith in Him isn't the absence of grief, doubt or complaint. Instead, it is voicing our anguish to the One who created us, who loves us and who can restore us.

When God called Moses to lead His people out of Egypt, He spoke to Moses from a bush that was burning, yet was not being consumed. God told Moses to take off his sandals, "for the place on which you are standing is holy ground" (Exodus 3:5).

The spot alongside the highway where Mark cried out to God wasn't a place where God called Mark to a special role, yet Mark perceives it as holy ground, as a spot where something pivotal in his pilgrimage happened, as a special place where God met him in a time of deep need. Twenty-four years later, Mark insists, "I can take you to that very spot where we pulled the car over."

The days ahead weren't easy, but three factors began to improve his mood: honest communication that enhanced the bond he had with the Lord; reviewing Bible promises he had memorized and the eventual stabilization of his brain chemistry. Mark experienced these truths: the Lord is "the One who lifts my head" (Psalm 3:3) and "My helper…the sustainer of my soul" (Psalm 54:4).

Winning at Warfare

Not every element in Mark's story can be contained in a single event nor lends itself to a precise chronology. For instance, learning to release his resentment, described previously in this chapter, was an episodic process that occurred both before and after his three-week stay in the hospital.

Similarly, though Mark's deep depression didn't occur until after he left the hospital, emotional ups and downs also characterized his hospital stay. Throughout the first couple of months after the accident, his emotional battles often evolved into spiritual fights. "The devil saw that I was physically and emotionally weak," Mark explains, "so he tried to take advantage of my vulnerability."

The battlefield where Mark typically faced the enemy was in the realm of thought or belief. Satan wanted him mired in the muck of negativism, bitterness and complaint.

The enemy tried to shift Mark's focus to the unfairness of his adversity, with the intent of inciting resentment toward God and the other driver. "Why did God allow this? Why did that driver cross the line?" Mark pondered.

Satan inspired morbid, unhealthy introspection through questions Mark asked himself, such as, "Did God allow this because of some sin or flaw in me? Was I not consecrated enough?"

When deep depression enveloped Mark, the devil would whisper, "This despair will never lift. God doesn't care about what's happening to you. In your condition, you will never fulfill any significant purpose."

How did Mark respond to these spiritual attacks? He didn't raise a white flag and surrender to the enemy's barrage of negativism. Here is where the benefit of knowing God's Word, also illustrated in Chapter 4, rescued Mark on the battlefield. Though Mark recommends that we should typically address our prayers to God, even during temptation, he believes there are times when God's people may address the evil one himself (as Jesus did in Matthew 4:1–11, right before He launched His public ministry).

When Satan predicted for Mark a bleak future, Mark answered, "Oh devil, 'God causes all things to work together for good to those who love God, to those who are called according to His purpose'" (Romans 8:28).

When the devil suggested that God had abandoned him, Mark countered with Hebrews 13:5: "Oh devil, God says, 'I will never desert you, nor will I ever forsake you.'"

When the enemy said that God would not restore him from this setback, Mark argued with a verse from Psalm 34:7: "The angel of the Lord encamps around those who fear Him, and rescues them."

"But the Lord is faithful, and He will strengthen and protect you from the evil one" (2 Thessalonians 3:3).

Due to Satan's persistence, spiritual warfare never ends in this life. Nonetheless, in the months subsequent to the accident, meditating on and wielding the sword of Scripture gradually instilled within Mark a more positive spirit. His wife and friends who visited saw more and more of Mark's trademark smile. He discovered firsthand that Satan flees when confronted with God's truth.

As the spring of 1996 progressed, Mark demonstrated a slow but noticeable improvement. On the other hand, he was still bedridden and a crucial deadline loomed. His dissertation had been accepted, but a few edits were needed. Final approval and receiving his diploma for the doctorate depended on a successful defense before the Dissertation Committee of West Virginia University.

He couldn't get an extension, not with all the committee members but one leaving or retiring after the spring semester. And he wasn't yet capable of traveling that far.

No matter how much tenacity he exercised, for this dilemma to be resolved in his favor Mark needed another instance of divine intervention. How could he tweak his dissertation, then successfully defend it, while immobilized in a hospital bed in his home?

Chapter 6

"CONGRATULATIONS, DR. SMITH!"

Y ou don't earn a college diploma and master's degree, then finish your doctorate by the age of 30, without dogged determination.

You don't tackle a taxing job as a hospital administrator, while simultaneously taking doctoral classes and pastoring a church, unless you're a high-energy leader who doesn't flinch when confronted by obstacles.

Because God had long-term leadership roles in mind for him, God hardwired Mark with an indomitable spirit. Then a near-fatal auto accident that put him flat on his back for a few months seemingly quashed his fearlessness and drive.

But only for so long.

During agonizing physical therapy sessions, his teeth-gritting exertion to wiggle his fingers and toes—the early stages of learning to walk again—demonstrated Mark's grit. The most dramatic exhibition of his pluck, though, occurred in the parking lot of a shopping mall in the late spring of 1996.

What did Mark do that left Debbie unhinged, furious at him?

Disabled Driver

Mark could finally move his legs a bit, but he couldn't walk unaided or without holding onto something sturdy. Occasionally getting out and about when Debbie ran errands was an enjoyable reprieve from household confinement.

Debbie entered the grocery store for a few items, leaving her one-year-old son safely tucked in his car seat and Mark nestled in the front passenger seat. Mark still wore the cumbersome external fixator on his left arm, which limited his movement. When Debbie exited the store and ambled toward her parking spot near the front entrance, what she saw—or in this case what she *did not* see—left her aghast.

"I looked up and saw that my car was gone!" Debbie recalls. "My heart began racing. My first thought was that someone had hijacked my car with my helpless son and husband still in it."

Then, from the far end of the parking lane, she spotted a familiar-looking car edging toward the front of the store where she stood. When the car got closer, "I recognized the face of my husband behind the wheel, grinning like he had just won the lottery.

"I ran up and opened the passenger door, yelling, 'What do you think you are doing!?'" Mark proceeded to tell Debbie that he had experienced a panic attack at the prospect of driving again. Abruptly, he decided that the only way to conquer that fear was to get behind the wheel. "I'm driving us home!" he announced.

To get in the driver's seat was no easy feat for Mark. He had to get on his feet at the passenger side, edge around the car sideways while holding onto the roof and hood, open the driver side door, then plop down behind the wheel.

But Debbie wasn't favorably impressed. "I'm not getting into this car with you driving!" she loudly proclaimed. "I'd rather walk home!" Mark kept insisting he was driving.

"Then I realized we were in a public place and people could hear my hysterics," Debbie admits. She didn't want observers to think a domestic violence incident was about to erupt, so to avoid embarrassment she reluctantly got in.

That incident exemplifies Mark Smith's disposition. His dauntless attitude keeps him from cowering before problems and limitations. "Even as a boy," Mark explains, "my parents said I was very determined. When it comes to obstacles, I don't give up easily. God gave me a fighting spirit." He acknowledges, "I don't sympathize with people who quit, who give up. My conviction is, 'With God's help, I'll win this battle!'"

Debbie admits that Mark's fortitude is a key to his effectiveness as a leader and was integral to his faster-than-expected recovery from the injuries. "What facilitated Mark's healing was his attitude," she admits.

Still, if she had it to do over again, one wonders if she would have left the car keys in the ignition at the shopping mall.

Defending the Dissertation

Let's back up a couple of months in time. Before Mark scared Debbie by driving for the first time since the accident, he faced another significant challenge.

After arriving home in late March from his three-week hospital stay, Mark faced the threatening deadline of a dissertation defense in April. The lingering physical discomfort and the negative effects of medicine he was still taking hampered his capacity to concentrate. An extension wasn't feasible. His dissertation committee chair from West Virginia University, Dr. John Andes, said to him, "Mark, we've got to get this done *now*. Four of your five committee members are retiring or leaving after this semester and if you wait you'll have to start all over."

"And those who know Thy name will put their trust in Thee; for Thou, O Lord, hast not forsaken those who seek Thee" (Psalm 9:10).

Mark understood what that meant: a long and tedious process of resubmitting his dissertation for approval by a different group of faculty. He desperately wanted to meet his goal of graduating in May. In light of his condition, how could this happen?

The first task, making the required edits to the dissertation, depended a lot on Debbie. Mark painstakingly went over it with her as she sat by his bed. While he verbalized the minor changes needed, she typed them.

The defense of the dissertation was the larger obstacle. Once again, God mobilized another person to be an agent of His grace for Mark. Dr. Andes, also a Christian, had been at WVU for 24 years. He visited the dean and received permission for an unconventional venue for the defense. He drove seven hours to Mark's house and set up a phone hookup with other members of the committee, so Mark could defend the dissertation from his bed. The defense required the physical presence of at least one committee member.

Defending a dissertation is no mental picnic. Committee members pose a lot of questions. You need razor-sharp thinking to justify your research methods and your findings. A positive outcome is far from automatic.

Due to the intensity of the interaction, as well as side effects of the medicine, "sweat was dripping off me during much of the defense," Mark recalls. What Mark said satisfied the committee. Two-and-a-half hours after the meeting started, Dr. Andes said the words that Mark longed to hear: "Congratulations, *Dr.* Smith!"

Drive for the Diploma

Despite impediments, Mark's tenacity enabled him to complete the dissertation process. The literal drive to the commencement in West Virginia would again test his mettle. Celebrating this milestone with his physical presence, made possible through the grace of God and others, was important to Mark.

Dr. John Andes, after congratulating Mark
on a successful defense of his doctoral dissertation.

Mark's dad visited Indiana with the intent of driving them to West Virginia, then down to his home state of Virginia to relax with family and friends. "We were all tense about how Mark would manage such a long trip," Debbie says. "Mark rode up front while Doug and I sat in back. You could tell Mark was apprehensive. If his dad hit the slightest bump in the road, it jostled Mark's bad arm and he'd ask his dad to improve his driving."

Then something happened to ramp up Mark's anxiety even more.

"Be anxious for nothing, but in everything by prayer and supplication with thanksgiving let your requests be made known to God" (Philippians 4:6).

They took an interstate exit to get gas. At the end of the exit ramp, a tractor-trailer, before turning, had edged too far out into the main road and needed to back up. The truck driver did not see the Smiths' car right behind him when he began backing up.

Debbie explains, "My father-in-law wasn't used to the gearshift in our car being in a different place, so he didn't react fast enough to keep from being hit by the truck. Our front end began crumpling and Mark started going to pieces. The truck was still edging backwards when I jumped out, yelling and flailing my arms to get the driver's attention.

"The damage to our car was minor and wouldn't keep us off the road. It took quite a while, though, to calm Mark down. The truck driver apologized profusely and we waited to fill out a police report."

That was precisely what Mark *didn't* need, an accident that ignited flashbacks to the horrific collision on March 3. Despite the anxiety over the incident, it didn't deter his resolve to keep going.

Since he could not walk up steps, school officials wheeled Mark to the front row of the auditorium, where they gave him his hood and diploma during the ceremony. "I was so proud of his accomplishment," Debbie exclaims, "but even more proud of his determination."

Five months after his near-fatal accident, Mark and Debbie Smith celebrated their 10th wedding anniversary. Grateful for his faster-than-expected recovery, Debbie wrote this poem to Mark as a gift.

TO MY HUSBAND ON OUR 10TH ANNIVERSARY

It's now been ten years
Since we first said our vows.
We promised to be faithful
And forsake all other guys and gals.
There's been lots of happy times
That we have shared,
And there's been the sad days
That together we have beared.

You're the same one I dreamed about
Many years ago.
The one I asked the Lord to send,
And He planned it so.
I cherish all the moments
We have had together;
Moments and memories
We'll hold dear forever.

Looking back over the years
I want you to know
I'm here to be with you
Wherever you go.
One thing for certain
I want you to hear:
I'd do it all over again
If you asked me this year.

Honey-bun, you're the one
That makes each day brighter,
The only one I want to hold me
Just a little tighter.
I want you to remember
These words without a doubt:
You're the only man in the world
Who I am crazy about.

From 1996 to 2005, Mark rose through the ranks of academic administration at Indiana Wesleyan University, finishing his tenure there as Vice President for Adult and Graduate Studies. Subsequently, he served as President of Ohio Christian University, where his initiatives resulted in a prodigious enrollment increase and far-reaching expansion of educational delivery systems.

In 2017, Mark became President of Columbia International University in South Carolina. His passionate leadership has already produced payoffs for CIU: increased donations, escalating enrollment, plus campus expansion and enhancements.

But to think that the effects of the 1996 accident are behind him would be a mistake. Before delving into more detail on how the Lord has favored Mark's leadership—and before explaining the irony of how he has succeeded not **in spite of** the accident, but **because** of it—the next chapter depicts his ongoing physical struggles and the effect on his faith.

Why is the deep well of God's grace, from which Mark gulped after the accident, still a tap from which he must drink daily?

Chapter 7

"IF I COULD GO JUST ONE DAY WITHOUT PAIN!"

What starts in the afternoon as a throbbing ache morphs into a burning sensation within a couple of hours. By eight p.m., he labels it a "roaring pain," as if an accelerant had been injected into the fire already glowing in his neck, left arm and hip. By 10:00 p.m., the ferocity of the pain generates tears.

This pain sequence is not the exception for Mark Smith; it is the rule. It doesn't describe an occasional rough day. Ever since the car crash in 1996, it's closer to a typical day. A number of times over the years, he has wished out loud to Debbie, "If I could just go one day without pain!" Yet his broken body won't let him. Debbie insists, "Most people who feel Mark's level of pain would go to the emergency room for relief."

In addition to the pain descriptors previously cited, how do the lingering effects of the accident limit Mark? What has he learned about handling pain in the midst of a challenging schedule? How can a man hurt this much and still serve as the high-profile president of two Christian colleges, where, by any measure, he has enjoyed extraordinary success?

In the final three chapters of his story, you will discover that Mark deflects the credit from himself and assigns it to the One who called and sustains him. You will see how his pain is a friend, not a foe. Your appreciation will escalate for a God who redeems pain for our good and for His glory.

Even if the suffering you experience is not physical, you will find help in this chapter.

Catalysts of Pain

What accounts for the persistent pain Mark experiences?

The thirteen screws that hold the bones of his hip together.

The two steel plates in his left arm, each held in place by several screws.

The large screw that, in effect, serves as his elbow, holding the bones of his forearm and upper arm together. Procedures to stimulate bone growth at his elbow, where he lost almost three inches of bone, were only partially successful.

Upper body movement, such as the gestures Mark employs when he speaks in public, exacerbates pain in and around a cyst in his spinal cord, in the neck. The accident caused a blood clot at this spot that doctors originally missed. Over time the clot evolved into a fluid-filled sac.

A change in barometric pressure also affects Mark's pain level. The barometric pressure is the weight of the air pressing against the earth's surface. That pressure rises and falls, depending on storms and shifts in weather. A person with severe joint injuries or disease can often feel a drop in barometric pressure before anyone observes a change in the weather.

A falling barometric pressure may increase pain by affecting the degree to which sacs of fluid lining the joints resists flow, or by triggering the pain receptors in the nerve endings of the joints. Put simply, many experts agree with grandma when she says, "I feel a storm comin'!"

Debbie calls Mark "the best weather forecaster I have ever met." The day before the second interview for this book, a severe storm rolled through the Midlands of South Carolina. Due to a sudden elevation of his pain, he predicted its arrival in advance.

Other factors that magnify Mark's physical pain include a high-stress day, inadequate sleep and excessive walking or standing. When his schedule calls for an evening engagement, he tries to lie down a while before dinner. The forms of exercise he best tolerates are biking and walking. He limits walks to twenty minutes or else it aggravates the hip pain. Recently, he committed to stretching the walk to 30 minutes for the sake of cardiovascular health, but he knows there will be a price to pay. Occasionally he swims, but the weaker left arm makes strokes a challenge. His left arm has less muscle mass and flexibility.

Perhaps discovering how he handles the daily pain will be more applicable to you.

Strategies for Pain Management

Mark has not found a secret elixir for relieving the pain.

His primary strategy to get through each day is desperate, heartfelt prayer. Daily, he seeks the Lord for the capacity to work and to relate to people while exhibiting a positive, optimistic spirit.

"Relying on the Lord isn't optional for me," Mark insists. "I regularly have to pray through the pain. I don't want to be a crotchety, complaining person, so I say, 'Oh Lord, keep me sweet.' At the start of the day, I whisper, 'Oh Lord, keep a smile on my face.' Then I tell myself, 'Today, I will smile!'"

"On the day I called Thou didst answer me; Thou didst make me bold with strength in my soul" (Psalm 138:3).

Mark can't control the pain, but he's convinced he can control his response to it. "It would be so easy to be self-centered when I'm hurting," he explains. "Yet attitude is a choice and I want my attitude to please the Lord. Negative, selfish thoughts often vie for my attention, but when they surface, I pray through them until God gives me a right attitude.

"Before the weaknesses caused by the accident," Mark continues, "I thought that I could accomplish a lot for Jesus, that I could make a difference and change the world. Though I loved the Lord and was serving Him in ministry, there was 'too much Mark Smith' involved in it. Then being flat on my back for months and with the pain that still badgers me daily, I realized that I am nothing, that it is only by His will and power that I was still living. To this day I am literally a needy, broken person who throws himself at the foot of the cross regularly.

"Without my frailty, I would probably be too self-sufficient. However, the brokenness prevents pride. Now, instead of thinking about what I can accomplish, my mindset is, 'Jesus, how can I serve You today? How can I give back to You for all You've done for me?'"

Mark sees himself in Matthew 5:3: "Blessed are the poor in spirit, for theirs is the Kingdom of heaven." He sees two benefits to his poverty of spirit. First, his frailty boosts his daily dependence on and intimacy with Christ. Second, awareness of his weaknesses means he is more prone to give the Lord credit when accomplishments occur.

A second way that Mark copes with the pain is medical intervention. Though Mark is careful not to take more than the prescribed dosage, he's grateful for medicine that temporarily reduces pain, especially when the throbbing surfaces during a day chock-full of presidential duties.

Despite Mark's primary reliance on prayer when he hurts, he sees medicine as a gift from God. He explains: "It's a fallacy to think we are being more spiritual if we rely solely on prayer. God has put the ingredients for medicines within His creation and He has given the apex of His creation—human beings—the capacity to create medicines. Using meds isn't at odds with prayer or with trusting God. It is taking advantage of a different form of His provision, a *common grace* that benefits mankind."

Another strategy when pain wells up is to focus more on the task at hand and on the people around him. "If I let my mind dwell on the throbbing of the pain, it seems to increase the intensity of it," Mark explains. "If I force myself to concentrate on the project I'm working on or the person I'm dealing with, I am less conscious of the discomfort. This phenomenon is even truer in relation to the despondency ongoing pain can cause. I've discovered that the quickest way through sadness or depression is *serving*."

Here are additional tips Mark has learned for muzzling the bite of the pain.

He drives to a wooded area for a brief walk. "The beauty of nature relaxes me," Mark notes. "Sometimes I go hunting, but I rarely shoot. Just enjoying the scenery soothes me."

When he isn't at the office working on the agenda for the day, he picks up a pen and writing pad and starts brainstorming. "I keep my mind busy by writing notes to myself, making lists of things to do in the future or by formulating new sermon ideas. A mental vacuum makes me more conscious of the pain."

He jots down goals for his personal life and ministry. He insists, "Envisioning what needs to happen in the future and focusing on obstacles to overcome so those things can be accomplished shift my focus off the pain. This goal setting especially helps when I'm in a despondent mood over the pain. The goals help me see a purpose for my life."

After a long trip or following an intense expenditure of energy in a short span of time, Mark allows his body to recuperate.

"I cannot overschedule or have too many things on my agenda following a trip involving speaking engagements, or logging extra hours in a week due to things like board meetings. Not only is a person's body trying to catch up, but I've observed that leaders are more vulnerable to Satan's attacks when they are exhausted. Recently, I spoke six times at a Bible conference in Alaska, then a few weeks later, represented Columbia International University in a trip to China. If I don't balance such output with rest I'm more likely to be irritable, negative and downcast."

In the spring of 2019, Dr. Smith participated in the first-ever graduation ceremony in China of Columbia Biblical Seminary's online Diploma of Chinese Mission program.

Mark also cites the need for a regular Sabbath rest, even if, for pastors, that is not on Sunday. "Weariness of body, mind and spirit increases vulnerability to despondency, even to temptation. Knowing we are more susceptible when our energy is depleted is a defense in itself. We can also have others pray for us at such times."

The human body always collects its debts. Inevitably, repayment takes time.

To complement these practical coping strategies, Mark also views his pain through the lens of a particular Bible truth.

Doctrinal Perspective on Pain

What enables Mark and Debbie to endure suffering is their rock-ribbed reliance on the sovereignty of God. This truth, both priceless and mysterious, avows that God plans and governs all things. Everything that has happened or will happen has been purposed by God. He governs natural as well as human events. Without a belief that God controls their circumstances, discouragement would overwhelm the Smiths.

As Debbie dealt with the immediate aftermath of the 1996 accident, she says, "My theme became, 'God allowed this to happen and now we'll have to trust Him to take care of us.' While Mark recuperated, I often quoted this to him." She didn't know *why* it had happened, but she felt comforted by *Who* governed what had happened.

"The Lord has established His throne in the heavens;
and His sovereignty rules over all" (Psalm 103:19).

Words he spoke about the lingering effects of the accident show that Mark anchors his thoughts on God's control over his life. "God chose me for this pain. That doesn't mean there aren't times when I want to be free of it, but it does mean I can trust Him to use it for good."

In a similar vein, Mark sees many Christians who cling to a shallow, unbiblical view of suffering. "They think that if they love God and follow Him, nothing bad will happen to them. Especially if they are a preacher or a missionary, they think God will shield them from pain. But that's false. I was in a head-on crash that wasn't my fault, right after giving what some members of the congregation had called an *anointed* sermon. This viewpoint on adversity doesn't take seriously enough the reality of living in a fallen world."

In our world, where sin is rampant and spiritual warfare rages, "Many are the afflictions of the righteous" (Psalm 34:19). *We should not expect on earth what God only promised for heaven.* Here is James I. Packer's sentiment on the mindset that assumes Christians can avoid affliction: "It confuses the Christian life on earth with the Christian life as it will be in heaven."[2]

Compassionate Outcome of Pain

For Mark and Debbie, one positive consequence of the accident is greater sensitivity to others who suffer. The ordeal foisted upon them in 1996, along with the ongoing pain Mark experiences, have increased their capacity to identify with others' suffering.

"Now I take a prayer request more seriously," Debbie contends, "whether it is for the person making it or someone that person loves. We relied so much on others' prayers, now

I'm more likely to follow through and pray when I hear or read a request." Receiving others' compassion enhances Debbie's capacity to give it.

Mark concedes that his hardship spurs him to apply Romans 12:15 more consistently. Paul admonished us to "rejoice with those who rejoice, and weep with those who weep." "My pain gives me *empathy* with others, not sympathy," Mark explains. "I better understand what they're going through. I'm more likely to encourage them."

His pain also expands his servant heart toward others even when they aren't suffering. As a visionary leader, Mark acknowledges that he is task-oriented and relentless in his pursuit of goals that will honor God and expand the university's impact. Typically, someone with his choleric temperament is inadvertently oblivious to needs of people with whom he works. Mark hasn't been immune to this tendency, yet over time his pastoral side has grown to match his goal-orientation. He has mellowed in how he relates to people.

The Chief Financial Officer at Columbia International University, Rob Hartman, has worked with Mark for over 18 years. In 2017, when Mark moved from Ohio Christian University to accept the presidency of CIU, Rob came with him. Rob sees in Mark a "strong mix of a Type A personality and a pastoral heart for people."[3]

In 2018, Mark appointed Dr. Andre Rogers, CIU Professor in Church Ministry, as a special assistant to the president's office. What Andre calls a "tender heart" is a trait he admires in Mark. "He cares about people. When someone he loves is mistreated or unfairly criticized, he is quick to come to their defense. People who hurt are drawn to him because they sense he really cares."[4]

On Mark's first official day in office at CIU, he walked to every office and workstation on campus, introducing himself to employees and getting their names. To compensate for salary increases that aren't yet as large as he yearns to give, several times a year, right before or after a paid holiday, he gives staff throughout the university one or more additional days off without a dock in pay. He isn't just trying to accumulate capital as a leader. It is a genuine expression of his concern for them and appreciation for their contributions to the ministry.

An exceptional sensitivity to pastors shows early every Sunday. He texts a large number of pastors, assuring them of his prayers for their sermon and worship service.

It is safe to say that Mark's broken body has softened his heart toward the Lord as well as toward other people. His pain accounts for a greater degree of compassion than he would otherwise exhibit.

Enhancing the pastoral dimension of Mark's leadership is one of the observable differences stemming from the accident. Chapter 8 expands on how God has blessed Mark's personal relationships. How has God's Spirit penetrated the dark providence of 1996 with a radiant light of favor on his personal evangelism? How has his painful experience increased his generosity and sensitivity to people in need?

Chapter 8

"I DON'T EVER WANT TO LOSE GOD'S FAVOR!"

From the world's vantage point, what the late pastor and author Ron Dunn said doesn't make any sense at all. Not in a culture that equates success with strength and associates productivity with human competence.

His words turn the world's value system on its head.

Even if you ask Christians, "What makes a person useful to God?," many of them refer to spiritual gifts or to God-given natural abilities. Others point to experience or to an excellent education. Certainly, some insist on sterling character as the primary prerequisite.

Few would cite Ron Dunn's answer to the question on usefulness.

But God's story line for His servants does not follow a script written by man. Perhaps Dunn was onto something when he said:

"God keeps a man usable by keeping him weak."[5]

Mark Smith is "Exhibit A" of Ron Dunn's remark.

You've already read descriptions and anecdotes of Mark's weakness: the broken, contrite spirit, generated within him by his helplessness following the accident, and the lingering pain that necessitates daily reliance on God's grace. Now the script of his story shifts to ways God has favored his life and leadership. To employ Ron Dunn's term, you will see how Mark is *more* "usable," not *less,* because of the accident.

Why was Mark's auto crash in 1996 not an intermission to the drama of his faith-fueled leadership, but an integral part of his life?

This chapter and the next answer that question. Chapter 8 highlights God's favor in Mark's personal relationships and effects on individuals. Chapter 9 reveals God's favor as a leader in three Christian universities.

What you read should help you realize that God can do more for and through *you* than you perhaps thought.

Understanding God's Favor

The concept of "God's favor" carries varied connotations.

There is a sense in which all of God's people enjoy the same degree of favor from God. He loves all of His children equally. Potentially, all who believe in Christ enjoy the same present and future benefits. Though God may discipline us through consequences of disobedience, our secure status with Him does not change. If we have put our faith in Christ, we don't move in and out of God's favor, for He accepts us on the basis of Christ's righteousness applied to us. His unconditional, persevering love for us does not change. We can't "lose" this kind of divine favor.

When I refer to God's favor on Mark's life and ministry, I am not implying an arbitrary divine favoritism or a level of fruitfulness available to no one else. I am simply acknowledging an observable reality: God has providentially and graciously chosen to give Mark extraordinary success.

"I entreated Thy favor with all my heart; be gracious to me according to Thy Word" (Psalm 119:58).

Not everyone with whom he has shared the gospel received Christ as Savior. Not every decision he makes as a leader spawns eyebrow-raising results. Nonetheless, it is clear that God has used him to change the lives of numerous individuals and the schools where he has served prospered under his leadership.

Mark learned to trust God in the crucible of pain. For the sake of God's honor and the spread of the gospel, the Lord rewards the faith Mark exercises. He isn't the first leader who has enjoyed exceptional favor in this sense and he won't be the last. Perhaps his brokenness and absolute surrender to God explain God's gracious choice to bless Mark's work to such an extent. If pride surfaces within a leader and he or she abandons daily dependence on the Lord, it is possible to lose this kind of favor.

Now let's proceed with ways in which God has blessed Mark's relationships with people, particularly concerning their relationship with Christ.

Perspectives on Illustrating God's Favor on Mark

In this chapter and the next, I'll share stories and statistics that show how the Lord has blessed Mark's personal and corporate ministries. As the writer of this book, I want you to know that I, not Mark, initiated the process of obtaining these evidences of his effectiveness. I posed interview questions that sought examples of God's favor on him. I researched articles about the CIU initiatives described in Chapter 9. Mark hesitated to talk about his success, fearing that the spotlight would shine too brightly on him.

Mark knows the stories and program initiatives I'll include depend on the working of God's Spirit. He realizes that an excellent team of coworkers is in large part responsible for the success at the three schools he has served.

When he finally agreed to talk about the ways God has favored him, he did so for this reason: "I want people to see how God can still use a weak, broken vessel. My hope is that broken persons who feel less useful to God due to a hardship will read this and get a glimpse of what God can do in and for and through them. Their roles may not be as public as mine or utilize the same spiritual gift package, but what God wants to do through them is no less consequential for His Kingdom."

Favor in Personal Ministry

When I asked Mark for examples of God's blessings on his ministry, his initial answers surprised me. I figured he would cite ways the three colleges where he has served blossomed in enrollment and program expansion. Instead, he told stories of his involvement with individuals. He did so with vigor and a beaming smile, speaking as much with his gestures as with his choice of words.

At the start of the day, Mark often prays, "Lord, show me someone to point to Christ today." The three stories that follow, representative of many others, show how God has answered this prayer.

Bedside Conversion

John, a bar owner, was as anti-religious as they come. He didn't know Christ. Folks who knew John warned Mark to stay away from him. Despite their warnings, Mark befriended John, repeatedly visiting him in his trailer. "It was the fourth or fifth visit before he let me pray for him," Mark recalls. "I think it was the ninth visit before I asked him if he knew Jesus. I wanted him to know I cared about him as a person."

Though John warmed up to Mark, he resisted the plan of salvation. Mark kept in touch with him even after a geographical move. Many years later, in his 70s, a heart attack felled John when he was already suffering from a different illness. In grave condition, he called Mark and said, "A man came into my hospital room wearing a clerical collar and wanted to give me last rites. But I want *you* to come. I'm ready. I want to know Jesus."

Mark adjusted his schedule as a college president and drove three hours to the hospital. He led John to Christ. Though feeble, John raised his arms and started praising the Lord.

Then John said, "I'm supposed to be baptized." In view of his physical condition, they didn't know if he would have the opportunity for a traditional baptism. His desire to be baptized prompted Mark to fill a cup with water and use it for an impromptu baptism ceremony in John's hospital room.

Several months later, John died. Mark preached his funeral. Mark put a cap on this conversion story by exclaiming, "*Isn't God good*?!"

"But to this one I will look, to him who is humble and contrite of spirit, and who trembles at My word" (Isaiah 66:2).

A former colleague at Ohio Christian University, Craig Brown, says, "Mark cares deeply for people." Referring to the auto accident, Craig explains that, "Mark's own mortality became very clear to him. He grasps how fragile life is and how quickly it can end." What Craig calls "an incredible sense of urgency" expresses itself in Mark's personal relationships and through evangelism, not just in his job-related sphere as a college president.[6]

Life Change at a Drive-Thru

It happened because Mark likes chocolate milkshakes. Only God could transform a fast-food restaurant's drive-thru into a sacred spot.

While President at Ohio Christian University, once a week Mark drove to get a chocolate milkshake for his lunch. He usually drove to the same place and interacted with the same young lady at the window. He treated her well, leaving a generous tip. It wasn't unusual to tell her to keep the change when he gave her a $10 bill for a $3 shake. He also kept telling her, only half-kidding, that she needed to leave the secular school she attended and enroll in a Christian college because, as he put it, "God has something special in mind for you!"

The Holy Spirt used Mark's kindness and challenge. Later, though she was not yet a Christian, she enrolled at OCU. Within the first month as a student there, she heard a chapel speaker explain the gospel and went forward to receive Christ as Savior.

Later on she told Mark her story, concluding, "Your persistence paid off! I want to thank you."

Their affiliation didn't stop with her attendance at OCU. She followed Mark and Debbie to Columbia International University when he assumed the presidency in the summer of 2017. She entered the M.A. program in Counseling.

Mark picks up her story: "She recently faced a horrible tragedy. I came to my office one day and found her there waiting on me, weeping. She said, 'Dr. Smith, I know you are the president and very busy, but I didn't know where else to go. I came to see you because I knew you loved me.' My staff and I prayed for her and reassured her of our support and love."

Mark continues, "I'm reminded that the Holy Spirit can use someone even at a drive-thru window. Wow, I love serving Jesus!"

Stop at a Tavern

Craig Brown disclosed another incident illustrating Mark's spontaneous relational ministry. Mark told the story to Craig years after it had happened, back when Mark had pastored a church in West Virginia. Mark was driving alone in his car when he drove by a tavern. He spotted a familiar car in the parking lot of the bar. The car belonged to a young man Mark knew who was going through a rough time.

Mark walked into the bar, sat by the young man and said, "Is this what you want your future to look like? There is no future for you in a place like this." Mark put his arm around him and led him outside. "I'm going to pray for you. You are going to rededicate your life to Christ," he told the young man.

According to Craig, Mark's boldness stems, at least in part, from physical frailty caused by the accident. "He knows he may have a short time to speak for God," Craig muses. "That makes him bolder, whether the occasion is a person's relationship with the Lord or raising the funds needed for a school project that will expand the institution's effectiveness."

Though this tavern incident occurred prior to Mark's 1996 accident, it reflects the sensitivity and attention to individuals that has only intensified due to the pain stemming from the crash.

Mark's lasting impact on people isn't limited to personal interventions like the ones we've seen in the three preceding stories.

Favor in Giving to People

To make a huge distinction between Mark's ministry to individuals and his broader realm of service in and through the schools where he has worked is impossible. To separate these forms of ministry would create a false dichotomy. That's because what Mark gives to these schools is, in effect, donations of his time, gifts, energy and funds *to the individuals who attend them.*

Though the ultimate recipient of all ministry is the Lord, Christian institutions exist to serve people, not vice versa.

A nice picture frame offers an attractive setting or border encasing portraits of beloved individuals. Similarly, a Christian college is the organizational framework that temporarily encloses the lives of precious students who grow in their faith and in their capacity to share it.

Here are just four examples of how Mark's leadership in, for and through schools has clearly coincided with his compassion for people.

Fundraising

Mark isn't shy about approaching individuals, heads of corporations or foundations for the monetary funds required to expand the Christian education of students. He asks boldly because he's asking for what will benefit students and ultimately, the spread of the gospel. Through Mark's efforts, God's Spirit has prompted others to donate many millions of dollars for Christian schools. The amount of money he has raised, combined with the entrepreneurial programming made possible by those funds, has generated over $200 million.

Demolishing Barriers

"I tend to pull for people who face barriers to reaching their potential," Mark says. "Due to my car accident, as well as my rural upbringing that didn't offer much financial privilege, God has given me a burden for the disadvantaged.

"This has prompted me to launch programs in African-American communities near the schools where I've served. I've reached into those communities in a variety of ways, but one very satisfactory outcome is the increase in educational opportunities. As a result of our initiatives over 25,000 African-American students have earned associates, bachelors, masters or doctoral degrees. This hasn't just improved *their* lives, it has quantitatively and qualitatively added to the Lord's labor force!"

Retreat Center

Mark and Debbie don't want to stop serving students when they graduate. They are especially interested in ongoing ministry to pastors. They know firsthand the unique pressures and spiritual warfare faced by pastors. A long-held dream of starting a Pastor's Retreat Center recently materialized. Through

December 2019, the house Mark obtained for this purpose hosted 13 pastoral couples.

Mark and Debbie Smith provide this home in Galax, Virginia as a place for rest and restoration for ministry couples.

New Churches

A Christian college isn't a provincial entity that competes with or eclipses in importance the local church. As a parachurch organization, a biblical university comes alongside churches, training men and women to assume staff positions and equipping missionaries to plant churches. That's why Mark gets personally involved by assisting in the launch of new congregations.

"God has helped us build two new churches," Mark shares enthusiastically, "one in Mexico and one in the United States."

"Therefore, my beloved brethren, be steadfast, immovable, always abounding in the work of the Lord, knowing that your toil is not in vain in the Lord" (1 Corinthians 15:58).

Please don't read the previous stories and statistics and put Mark Smith on a pedestal. He's eager to share his faith in Christ because, when he struggles to finish a day riddled with pain, he knows from experience how precious intimacy with Christ is and how sustaining His grace is. He realizes how vital a relationship with Christ is for the *present*, not just for eternity. He knows he would be less sensitive to others' needs if his body and spirit had not been broken by the collision.

A master carpenter uses solid wood to craft beautiful, intricate pieces of furniture. The varied instruments he uses to shape the wood don't claim credit for his achievement. Similarly, Mark is painfully aware that the credit for these achievements I've cited goes to the Lord. Mark may be His tool to help shape people and colleges, but he knows that the One who holds and employs the instrument deserves the acclaim.

Mark doesn't take God's ongoing favor for granted. He keeps praying, "*Lord, please help me to never, ever lose your favor.*"

Receiving Leads to Giving

Perhaps one reason Mark is a useful instrument is the love he has received over the years.

During his long recovery in 1996, you've read how the Lord expressed love to Mark by answering his pleas for sleep, for ending the nightmares about being trapped in the car and by providing emotional sustenance. He also blessed Mark with an extraordinary awareness of the Holy Spirit's presence. In addition, members of the family of God loved Mark and Debbie through their prayers, as well as through material provision and their own presence.

No wonder Mark has lots of love to give!

Perhaps *you* have more love to give than you thought, because of all the love you have received.

Mark's painful setback in 1996 didn't just increase his love for people and his concern for their eternal destiny. It has also left an indelible mark on how he leads as a university president. Mark asserts, "The accident made me the leader I am today."

How can that be true? The final chapter in Mark's story discloses the answer.

Chapter 9

"NOWHERE TO LOOK BUT UP!"

Perhaps no one is quoted on the subject of leadership more often than best-selling author John Maxwell. Here is one of his best-known statements: "If you think you are a leader, yet no one is following you, you are only taking a walk."[7]

Mark Smith isn't known for taking solitary walks.

Typically, when Mark communicates vision, members of his team and other stakeholders receive it enthusiastically. He galvanizes support for it, as others start seeing the same landmarks on the horizon that Mark sees.

Two administrators who have worked alongside Mark are effusive in talking about the hand of God upon Mark's academic leadership. Rob Hartman, who has served with Mark for over 18 years, says, "There is a sense of God's anointing on him.

I don't know what else to call it. That's why I want to work with him." Craig Brown adds, "The favor of God rests on Mark, because He has used him so mightily."

In his role at three Christian colleges, what are some evidences of God's favor? What accounts for that favor?

What you learn will tell you more about the Lord than it does about Mark.

Indiana Wesleyan University (1996–2005)

Mark believes that he should "attempt things that only *God* can accomplish."

He derives this visionary concept in part due to a Bible verse that buoyed his spirit during recovery from the car accident, which occurred less than three months after Mark started his job as Assistant Faculty Dean. Despite a bleak prognosis from doctors and uncertainty about the viability of future employment, he kept clinging to Luke 1:37: "Nothing will be impossible with God."

In the three positions he held at IWU, his initiatives helped to expand enrollment and educational programs. I've selected only a few examples from his years there.

- He assisted in the development and implementation of six new programs in the College of Adult and Professional Studies.
- In the same division of the university, Mark managed the implementation of seven new online programs.
- Mark led the team that gained approval of the first-ever doctorate at IWU.

- As Vice President of Graduate and Adult Studies (2001–2005), he launched a strategic plan that increased enrollment in those colleges from 5,000 to 10,000.

Clearly, God had equipped Mark for what He had called him to do at IWU. He identifies with Paul's declaration in 2 Corinthians 3:5: "Not that we are adequate in ourselves to consider anything as coming from ourselves, but our adequacy is from God."

A former colleague of Mark's who still serves at IWU, Elvin Weinmann, points out, "The accident left Mark totally dependent on others during the recovery process. While some people gave up on the prospect that Mark would ever again be gainfully employed, he was at a point where he had nowhere to look but up. He looked to God, learned to walk again, and ever since God has marvelously blessed his academic leadership."[8]

Nowhere to look but up. Now that's a strategic vantage point!

Ohio Christian University (2006–2017)

Five simple words aptly summarize Mark's zeal for leadership: "I like to grow things."[9] That was extremely evident when he wielded the presidency of OCU.

While Mark served at OCU, a new chapel facility became a dire need. Mark's go-for-it attitude infected those who worked with and for him. "Let's do it!," he said, in reference to the chapel. He recognized that such grand plans require far more than merely human endeavor. "I called for a 40-day period that involved fasting and earnest prayer," he recalls. "The Holy Spirit needed to be involved in every phase of the project, starting with prompting donors to give the necessary funds."

Mark tells what happened next.

"One man walked into my office on a Saturday morning and pledged $1 million. I flew to Dallas to visit a man who, to this day (2020), has not visited the OCU campus. He gave $500,000. I returned home excited and talked to my wife about the good start to the fundraising. My eight-year-old son, Micah, overheard my comments about funds for the chapel project. When Debbie put Micah to bed and prayed with him, the Holy Spirit spoke to his heart. He told her, 'Mom, I have $37 in my piggybank. I've been saving for a bicycle, but I want to give it for the chapel.'

"Our hearts were touched! Days later, I took Micah's piggybank with me as an object lesson to a fundraising event for the chapel. Realistically, we expected to procure about $100,000 in donations at that event. I told them Micah's story and they gave $600,000! The Lord took Micah's gift and multiplied it, just as He did with the boy's gift of loaves and fishes in the New Testament.

"I didn't know what to say except, '*Wow, God*!'"

Within three months, donors had pledged $5 million! "That was a chapel built by the faith of God's people," Mark explains, "including the faith of a little boy."

How could Mark approach such a challenging project with optimism?

"I had seen God answer desperate prayers from my hospital bed in 1996," Mark reminisces. "He met our financial needs, directly answered a plea for sleep and an end to nightmares, and promoted healing in my body to a far greater extent than doctors expected. That imbued me with the capacity to trust Him for more as the years went by, especially when it came to funding for projects that I thought would honor God and enhance a school's ministry. *The trauma in 1996 made me a man of prayer and faith.*

"I kept wanting God to do *more,* because of what I had seen Him do in the past. My faith increased incrementally as I kept accumulating memories of His past faithfulness."

"But if any of you lacks wisdom, let him ask of God, who gives to all men generously and without reproach, and it will be given to him" (James 1:5).

Here are several other ways God blessed OCU during Mark's presidency:

- The launch of 14 new learning sites in rural areas of the state.
- Raising $30 million in capital funds, with a $3 to 4 million operational excess.
- Enrollment explosion from 400 to 4,600 students in 10 years.

Again, Craig Brown contributes an insight about Mark's leadership, calling him a "very focused, intentional, visionary leader. When he believes a particular initiative will honor God and help the ministry, he sinks his teeth into it with bulldog tenacity. He doesn't let go."

Craig is quick to point out that Mark's leadership is far from autocratic. "Mark prays hard for God to reveal *His* will to him. Next, he bounces the idea off the president's cabinet and other advisors. If they catch the vision, Mark moves speedily to accomplish it."

Craig views Mark's success as a derivative of his close walk with the Lord. "He's constantly in the Word of God," Craig says. "He often tweets Bible verses to friends all over the country, sharing truths that ministered to him that morning. 'Here's a verse for you,' Mark says, wanting what encouraged or challenged him to exert the same effect on his friends. When I worked with him, it was also pretty common to hear Mark singing a hymn as he entered a meeting or during a lull in our conversation when we were in a car."

Alluding to Mark's daily pain stemming from the crash, Craig explains, "Mark sees the Lord as his moment-by-moment sustainer. He realizes, to a degree greater than before the collision, 'I can do nothing on my own.' Mark sees each day as a new lease on life, so he faces it optimistically and with a greater sense of purpose. His sense of urgency makes him less reticent when it comes to casting vision, making decisions or offering proposals for change. He doesn't fear failure because he knows God is capable of providing and sovereign over outcomes that don't materialize like he hoped."

"For it is God who is at work in you, both to will and to work for His good pleasure" (Philippians 2:13).

Craig also said, "When Mark Smith moves to a new position, neither the school nor the community will ever be the same."

A glance at Mark's first two and a half years as President of Columbia International University reveals the accuracy of Craig's words.

Columbia International University (2017–)

The entrance to CIU's 400-acre campus in Columbia, South Carolina. Photo by Seth Berry.

Some people associate leadership with the spotlight, with a privileged status, even with glamor that isn't typically true in the realm of the Spirit. For a *Christian* leader—whether the venue is a church, parachurch organization or a school—the job description often comes wrapped in a burden.

When the CIU Board of Trustees appointed Mark to the presidency in 2017, Mark was keenly aware of the school's outstanding reputation in Christian education. He knew CIU has an enduring legacy of producing exceptional vocational Christian workers who blanket the globe, as well as an increasing number of ministering professionals in the marketplace.

The board's primary mandate to Mark was, "Grow enrollment." He saw the responsibility as serious business laden with eternal consequences. He did not assume success just because God had favored his leadership at two other colleges.

That's why, prior to taking office July 1, 2017, Mark launched a 30-day period when he personally engaged in intense prayer, seeking God's will for the school. At this pivotal time in the school's history, he sought the Lord for strategies that would prove integral to qualitative and to quantitative growth. He prayed repeatedly, "Lord, what is *Your* vision for CIU?"

Mark wrestled with God for a sense of direction so he could hit the ground running on July 1. He needed a decisiveness rooted in a divinely inspired vision. The burden for the school's future kept him awake many nights. He'd get out of bed and walk the floor, pleading with God for ideas and direction.

Debbie expressed concern for Mark's health. "If you don't get more rest, you're going to have a heart attack!" she told him.

As ideas prompted by the Lord began to coalesce in his mind, Mark wrote them down. Gradually, certain priorities took visible form in his thinking. He outlined a one-page document that put his initial vision into concrete form. I'll elaborate on two of his initiatives.

Business and Information Technology

The primary initiative he believes God gave him was the construction of a business and information technology center to help fulfill CIU's mission. He could see it in his mind: a state-of-the-art facility erected near the entrance to CIU.

He wondered how his advisors in the president's cabinet would receive an idea that could cost close to $20 million. How would board members react to such a costly strategy? Being new to this school, would he be able to cast a vision that attracted donors who did not yet know him personally?

Before he explained his idea to others, Mark's humanness showed in remarks he made to Debbie: "I believe God gave me this idea, but I'm scared to death. I may make a fool of myself when I share this."

When he shared it with members of the president's cabinet, Mark painted a picture of the future that they, too, could envision. They bought into it. Board members who heard the plan also caught Mark's infectious enthusiasm for it. He received a green light to proceed.

Another early initiative integral to the new facility was to complete and to market fully online undergraduate and graduate degrees in Business. The work of those students would soon be generated from the new facility. Efforts to raise the necessary funds began in earnest.

Within six months, Mark and his team raised $16 million in donations for the business and IT initiative. One donor family, who owns a thriving business and has long been a friend of CIU, wept for joy when Mark shared his vision concerning how business could be a vehicle for fulfilling CIU's mission. That family gave a huge boost to the vision with a $12 million pledge.

In late summer of 2019, the William H. Jones Global Business and IT Center opened its doors. What inspired the name is the ministry of Bill Jones, current CIU Chancellor and former president of the school. For years, Bill has led Bible studies for businessmen and he has led many of them to faith in Christ.

"Not to us, O Lord, not to us, but to Thy name give glory because of Thy lovingkindness, because of Thy truth" (Psalm 115:1).

The IT component will dramatically enhance the campus IT functionality and infrastructure for all CIU students and staff. Students in the Business and Organizational Leadership program will directly benefit. Scott Adams, director of this program, speaks to the timeliness of the Center: "The global marketplace is the next great wave of effective evangelism and discipleship. The Center will be a hub for equipping students who will serve in Christian organizations, including mission agencies. Many students will also serve as ministering professionals in businesses, health care facilities and cross-cultural organizations."[10]

With a vision beyond CIU's campus, the Center will also offer training for Columbia area professionals, persons who want to learn how to launch new businesses or receive ongoing professional development. In addition, it will provide a high school "Young Professional Business/IT Academy" for the students of Ben Lippen School, CIU's Pre-K to 12th grade Christian school.

The William H. Jones Global Business and IT Center opened in August, 2019.

Community Revitalization

When Mark casts a vision for a school, he isn't provincial in his outlook. In his peripheral vision, he also sees needs of nearby neighborhoods.

A two-mile stretch of highway connecting CIU's campus with a nearby interstate was known for its deteriorating buildings, trash and escalating crime. Early in his CIU tenure, in a one-week period of time, law enforcement responded to eight different calls close to the campus.

Aided by pastors of nearby churches, especially Andre Melvin and Andre Rogers (also CIU faculty members), Mark became a catalyst for community enhancement. He met with church and civic leaders, along with concerned citizens, to discuss the problem.

Then Mark acted, raising $1.5 million in private donations to purchase seven blighted properties. Abandoned buildings were demolished and the lots cleared of debris. By the spring of 2019, the partnership between CIU and neighborhood leaders in this northern section of Columbia reached a milestone that will transform decaying properties into commercially viable places. The outcome will be enhanced appearance, greater safety and new businesses to improve the area's economy.

According to Mark, "A strong core value of CIU is giving back to the community. As we take Christ to the nations, we must start at home."[11]

Initial goals included additional lighting along the corridor and an increased law enforcement presence. The plans for community revitalization dovetail with the new William H. Jones Business and IT Center. One of its purposes is to train local professionals on how to start and to manage a successful business.

At a news conference announcing this revitalization project, Columbia Mayor Steve Benjamin said, "The potential of this region of the city is immense. Anyone who doesn't see what's happening with CIU's incredible infrastructure investment is going to miss the boat. This is an opportunity, not a challenge."[12]

Columbia's mayor, police officers, local pastors, and Dr. Smith were among those participating in the news conference announcing the community revitalization project, facilitated by CIU's infrastructure investment.

Mark realizes that continued revitalization will require help from groups and persons who have no affiliation with CIU, as well as funding by local government agencies. Yet he was originally confident that he would eventually see new businesses such as a gas station, a bank, a pharmacy or a fast-food restaurant dot the landscape. By late summer of 2019, that confident vision began to materialize. CIU entered into an agreement with Jones Petroleum of Georgia for a Dairy Queen restaurant/convenience store combination, the first new business establishment planned for the Monticello Road corridor to the CIU campus. By late 2019, the police also manned a new regional headquarters along this corridor.

The North Columbia Business Association gave CIU the 2019 "Community Impact Organization of the Year Award" for the improvements on the Monticello Road corridor between the campus and Interstate 20. Dr. Smith accepted the award for CIU at the January 2020 Mayor's Roundtable Luncheon.

"Resources always follow vision," Mark asserts. Now the vision is not just Mark's. A growing number of community leaders own it as well.

Another significant indicator of God's blessings on Mark's leadership at CIU concerns enrollment. During his first five semesters as president, enrollment escalated 53% (through fall 2019 semester). He also spearheaded a number of campus improvement projects, raising $2.5 million toward a $4 million expansion and enhancement of the cafeteria. (*For an update on academic programs and happenings at CIU, see the contact information at the back of this book.*)

When Mark considers the positive changes inspired by his leadership at the three universities, he is adamant about one thing: *God did it!* He insists, "No amount of human effort alone will ever accomplish Kingdom results."

As long as Mark's passion remains the accomplishment of *God's* will, rather than his own personal agenda, and as long as his heart stays fixed on the Lord, he won't lose the favor of God on his ministry.

Top Billing

Many years ago, movie theatres erected a large marquee on the street near the entrance. There, in an effort to entice people to see the movie, they put the title in large letters, along with the names of a couple of lead actors or actresses. Not every well-known actor in the movie made the marquee. The person whose name appeared first was the one with the most public appeal or renown. Top billing meant you had arrived as an actor. You were the biggest star appearing in the show.

In Mark Smith's story, *Jesus Christ deserves top billing.*

"But we have this treasure in earthen vessels that the surpassing greatness of the power may be of God and not from ourselves" (2 Corinthians 4:7).

Please leave his story with a positive impression of Mark's Savior and sustainer, not of Mark Smith. And mull over the implications of Mark's story for your own pilgrimage as a Christian.

What the Lord has done for Mark speaks not only to the person with chronic pain or a disability, but to the emotionally weak, or to those whose motivation to keep going has been smothered by a keen disappointment or difficultly. It says something to the one whose brokenness has siphoned off confidence that God can use him or her in the church or community.

Does this include you? If you lean in and cup your ears, what is God's Spirit saying to you right now? Why should Mark's story inject hope and optimism concerning your future usefulness?

I've tried to show through Mark's story that in the reverse logic of God, the people most useful to Him are the ones who've come to the end of themselves. That those with big faith for ministry initiatives are persons who've learned to rely on Christ during big setbacks.

That what many call hindrances to usefulness are, in disguise, divine opportunities.

That God's dark providence in the lives of His people can spread the light of the gospel even farther, rather than obscuring that light.

That God may get more glory by redeeming our pain, rather than by eradicating it.

Oh, what divine ironies!

The way up with God is down.

The strongest Christian is the one who acknowledges his or her weakness.

The most useful vessels in the Lord's hands are the cracked ones.

The ones who serve best in God's army are the wounded soldiers.

The leader with the most authority for good is the one who has bowed to a Higher Authority.

Dwight L. Moody said, "The world has yet to see what God will do with and for and through and in and by the man who is fully consecrated to Him."[13] If Mark Smith has a secret to his success, that's it. The key words in Moody's quote are "*what God will do.*" The Giver of grace gets the glory, not the recipient of His grace.

The jury is in and the verdict is: *if you're in pain, fragile or needy—if desperate dependence on Christ is necessary just to get you through each day—then you are a prime candidate for reaping eternal dividends.*

Mark's story can be yours, in whatever sphere of influence God has put you.

As I reflect on Mark's story, a remark Paul made in 1 Corinthians 15:10 comes to mind. "By the grace of God I am what I am, and His grace toward me did not prove vain." God's grace toward Mark has not been in vain, either.

God speaks through pain and He does not stutter!

Soli Deo gloria. Glory to God!

Part 2 of the book identifies timeless faith lessons rooted in the narrative you've finished. I will explain encouraging biblical principles and help you apply them to your life and ministry. Even if you do not see yourself as a leader, or if your difficulty isn't a physical infirmity, these insights apply to your life as a follower of Christ.

PART 2
FAITH LESSONS

PERSPECTIVES TO HELP GOD'S PEOPLE DEAL WITH PAIN AND SUFFERING

The chapters in Part 2 beam the spotlight on principles or biblical perspectives gleaned from Mark's story. Each insight surfaced in at least one of the story chapters, either in remarks made by Mark or Debbie or in a description of story elements. In Part 2, I will isolate ten insights, expand on each and offer ways to enhance your personal application of it.

The format facilitates using each Faith Lesson as a devotional. Implementing the application suggestions will increase the likelihood of life change in relation to each theme.

Here is the three-step format for each Faith Lesson:

Approach the Word

You'll read an anecdote, quote or other life-related introduction that grabs your attention and whets your appetite for the material that follows.

Absorb the Word

You'll receive a review and elaboration of the principle that help you to absorb it fully into your mind. The quotes, Scripture and commentary activate the turning of your mental gears, allowing you to process the biblical principle and its implications. Some lessons contain remarks by Mark or Debbie not included in the story section and references to Scripture not necessarily cited in the story. Each truth applies to the life of every reader, not just to the Smiths.

Apply the Word

This section may offer Bible study questions on one or more selected passages, so you can hear directly from the Holy Spirit on the lesson theme. Or, I may suggest other personal responses to help you apply the principle. In some cases, I recommend resources on the lesson theme. The ultimate goal is that you will put feet to the principle and run with it, so it moves beyond the printed page.

Faith Lesson 1
CLINGING TO GOD'S WORD

"Within the Scripture there is a balm for every wound, a salve for every sore." [14]

—Charles H. Spurgeon

Approach The Word

What is the most memorable sermon you've ever heard? Why did it leave an indelible impression?

When is the last time a sermon encouraged you, supplying the Holy Spirit's comfort and instilling hope during a time of discouragement?

Sound biblical preaching is integral to a church's health. Sermons point listeners to the provision of the cross for dealing with sin, instill a God-centered worldview, enable folks to win at spiritual warfare, facilitate godly choices and enhance love for our Savior.

Despite the necessity of good preaching in pulpits, the most profitable sermons you'll ever hear aren't the ones others deliver. *The most sin-defeating, hope-instilling, faith-sustaining sermons you'll ever hear are the ones you preach to yourself!*

In the difficult months following his near-fatal accident, Mark and Debbie Smith modeled this truth.

Absorb the Word

Mark's story described and illustrated how the spiritual sustenance he and Debbie received relied in large part on the Bible texts they "preached to themselves." Clinging to God's Word kept them fastened to their faith in Christ.

They kept giving biblically informed rebuttals to negative thoughts and to outright lies of Satan. Bible texts they had memorized, or with which they were very familiar, enabled them to "talk back" to the despair that often accompanied his accident and the long months of recovery.

When Mark's future looked bleak, when pain rifled through his body, when hopelessness settled in, when they battled resentment over the unfairness of the affliction and when Satan took advantage of their vulnerability to whisper untrue things about God, they meditated on God's Word to provide perspective and emotional equilibrium.

Chapters 4–5 showed how specific texts kept the Smiths focused on the character and promises of God. For example, when doctors kept delivering a bleak prognosis for the future, Mark kept telling himself, "Nothing will be impossible with God" (Luke 1:37). When Debbie's thoughts zeroed in on the difficult challenges they faced, she reminded herself of Psalm 121:1–2: "I will lift up my eyes to the mountains, from whence shall my help come? My help comes from the Lord, who made heaven and earth."

You read the details of how these additional texts were ones that anchored Mark's faith: Psalm 34:1–7, Romans 8:28 and Philippians 4:13. You saw how God's Spirit buoyed Debbie through the remaining verses in Psalm 121, as well as through Psalm 91 and Isaiah 30:15. These passages represented many more that they preached to themselves, which became rays of bright light that broke through the dark clouds hovering over them.

Mark and Debbie showed what fueled the faith necessary for handling trials. According to Romans 10:17, "Faith comes by hearing, and hearing by the word of Christ."

They applied a faith lesson that every believer has heard, many Christians have taught, but fewer have learned out of sheer desperation and necessity.

Key Truth

The truths and promises in God's Word encourage a hurting person and fuel trust in the Lord for handling even the most agonizing circumstance.

Apply the Word

To receive the Bible's encouraging perspectives and strength requires thorough acquaintance with it.

We obtain the requisite knowledge through our pastor's preaching, participation in Bible study groups and our personal quiet times. A specific discipline that expedited the Smiths' capacity to recall pertinent Scripture was a long-held habit of memorizing verses. Add regular memorization to the other venues for learning and our Bible knowledge rapidly escalates.

Of special value for persons going through difficult times is memorizing the promises in God's Word. Most of the passages the Smiths cited contained timeless promises.

According to 2 Peter 1:4, divine promises are essential to facilitate Christlikeness and purity: "He has granted to us His precious and magnificent promises, in order that by them you might become partakers of the divine nature, having escaped the corruption that is in the world by lust."

The late Dallas Willard, renowned author and scholar, insisted, "Bible memorization is absolutely fundamental to spiritual formation. If I had to choose among all the disciplines of the spiritual life, I would choose Bible memorization, because it is a fundamental way of filling our minds with what they need."[15]

The following verses offer more soul-nourishing promises to God's people when they suffer. Add these to the selections that massaged Mark's and Debbie's hearts.

"Why are you in despair, O my soul? And why have you become disturbed within me? Hope in God, for I shall yet praise Him, the help of my countenance, and my God" (Psalm 42:11).

"Do not fear, for I have redeemed you; I have called you by name; you are Mine! When you pass through the waters, I will be with you; and through the rivers, they will not overflow you. When you walk through the fire, you will not be scorched, nor will the flame burn you" (Isaiah 43:1–2).

"And after you have suffered for a little while, the God of all grace, who called you to His eternal glory in Christ, will Himself perfect, confirm, strengthen, and establish you" (1 Peter 5:10).

"He shall wipe away every tear from their eyes; and there shall no longer be any death; there shall no longer be any mourning, or crying, or pain" (Revelation 21:4).

- Which of these verses resonates most with you right now? Why?
- Which of these verses reminds you most of Mark Smith's story? Why?
- Which of these verses is God's Spirit nudging you to memorize this week?

Resource

The most comprehensive Bible memory program I'm aware of is at *fighterverses.com*. Bethlehem Baptist Church, where John Piper pastored for many years, launched this program consisting of 52 verses a year for five years. You can obtain small packets containing sets of verses or download them on an app. The general purpose is to help believers "fight the fight of faith." You can also access the information by googling, "Bethlehem Baptist Church Bible Memory Program."

Faith Lesson 2

PLEADING WITH GOD

"Prayer is not overcoming God's reluctance. It is laying hold of God's willingness." [16]

—Martin Luther

Approach the Word

I once heard a Christian insist that the more mature we become in the faith, the less we will ask God for and the more we will thank and praise Him.

It isn't the call for more praise and thankfulness that bothers me. Gratitude for what God does and praise for who He is are integral to a vibrant personal relationship with Him. What unsettled me was his suggestion that we are less spiritual if we consistently petition God for something.

Richard Foster, a prolific author who is highly respected for his views on spiritual formation, balks at the statement, too. He elaborates on the importance of pleading with God:

> Some have suggested that while the less discerning will continue to appeal to God for aid, the real masters of the spiritual life go beyond petition to adoring God's essence with no needs or requests whatever. In this view, our asking represents a more crude and naïve form of prayer.
>
> This, I submit to you, is a false spirituality. Petitionary prayer remains primary throughout our lives because we are forever dependent upon God. It is something that we never really "get beyond."[17]

Long before the life-altering car accident at age 30, Mark Smith had cultivated a habit of boldly asking God for personal and ministry needs. Then, after the accident, he took "pleading with God" to an even higher level.

How did the accident and its aftermath ramp up Mark's prayer life? Why is asking or pleading with God patently not a lower form of prayer? How do our petitions provide a means of revealing God's glory?

Absorb the Word

Mark's Persistent Petitions

Though Mark regularly offered faith-inspired prayers to God during his first 30 years, he learned the most about prayer and faith from his hospital bed. The combination of horrific pain, a bleak long-term prognosis, poor sleep and nightmares led to impassioned pleas for God's help. In a request for more sleep and an end to nightmares about the wreck, he cried, "I'm so tired of this, Lord. Will You do this for me?" God answered affirmatively that very night.

Weeks later, during his recovery at home, perhaps his lowest moment was learning he would need another arm surgery and hospital stay. Returning from the doctor visit, he asked Debbie to pull off the road, where he cried and lamented, "Oh God, I can't take this anymore! I can't face another surgery!" He learned to express his discouragement and complaint to the One he loved the most.

You also read how Mark and Debbie recognized a tinge of bitterness developing because the accident had not been Mark's fault. They both confessed their resentment and asked God for the strength to forgive. When Mark experienced a month-long depression precipitated by going off the powerful pain meds, Mark refuted Satan's attempts to take advantage of his vulnerable state. He pleaded with God and quoted Scripture to himself—and to Satan—to refute Satan's efforts to make him more negative and bitter.

More recently, due to the ongoing pain described in Chapter 7, daily pleas for sustenance have been Mark's primary means of coping. He says, "Relying on the Lord's strength each day is an absolute necessity for me. The only way I can exhibit a positive, optimistic attitude while I work and relate to people is to pray through the pain."

When Mark seeks God's wisdom as a college president and boldly asks God to provide the funds required by new program initiatives, he realizes that the classroom where he learned to ask God for big things was a hospital bed where he lay with a broken body and spirit.

All of Mark's pleading with God has increased his intimacy with the Lord and has fueled within him more prayers of gratitude and praise.

Biblical Precedents for Pleading with God

God's Word consistently invites or commands us to take our needs to Him in prayer. Both the Old and New Testament brim with appeals to petition God. The four texts that follow represent scores of others that extend such an invitation.

Psalm 55:22: "Cast your burden upon the Lord, and He will sustain you."

Jeremiah 33:3: "Call to Me, and I will answer you, and I will tell you great and mighty things which you do not know."

Matthew 11:28–29: "Come to Me, all who are weary and heavy-laden, and I will give you rest. Take My yoke upon you, and learn from Me, for I am gentle and humble in heart; and you shall find rest for your souls."

Philippians 4:6–7: "Be anxious for nothing, but in everything by prayer and supplication with thanksgiving let your requests be made known to God. And the peace of God, which surpasses all comprehension, shall guard your hearts and minds in Christ Jesus."

Which of these invitations to pray resonates most with you today? Why?

Pleading for God's intervention provides an opportunity for Him to receive more glory. In Psalm 50:15, there is a direct grammatical link between the outcome of honoring God, and calling upon Him with our needs: "Call upon Me in the day of trouble; I shall rescue you, and you will honor Me."

The root concept of the Biblical noun "glory," or the verb, "to glorify," is *weight*. God is *heavy* in the figurative sense of significance, importance or majesty.

When we are needy or inadequate, we're prompted to pray due to the limits of our resourcefulness and the press of outside forces. Then God answers and displays His power in some manner. He fortifies us or alters circumstances and we praise Him and tell others what He did. Being at our wit's end magnifies His name because He gets a chance to be God, to do what only He can do.

John Piper's take on Psalm 50:15 affirms this perspective. "We glorify God not so much by serving Him, but by being served by Him…We do not glorify God by serving His needs, but by praying that He would provide for ours, and trusting Him to answer. The Giver gets the glory. We get help."[18]

Also commenting on Psalm 50:15, Charles Spurgeon wrote, "We shall bring our Lord most glory when we get from Him much grace."[19]

If you feel a deep need for God's grace today, be encouraged!

What are the implications of these biblical precedents for your own prayer life?

Key Truth

A means of grace for handling adversity or for any kind of need is petitioning God through prayer. In His Word, God repeatedly invites us to ask Him for help. He receives glory when He answers our pleas.

Apply the Word

An Invitation

What is the Holy Spirit prompting you to ask God for today?

Whether you face a life-changing circumstance like Mark did or you think your need pales in comparison, go to the Lord with it today. In a *Family Circus* cartoon, Dolly overhears her little brother sitting on his bed, praying. She says, "It's okay to ask God for little things, Jeffy. *Everything is little to God*!"[20] The habit of asking Him for what you consider small things predisposes you to go to Him when your need or suffering is significant.

For Additional Study

If you want to study a Bible passage on the theme of pleading with God, examine Psalm 143 in light of these questions. Look for what King David implied, as well as what he directly stated.

- What words from the text describe *how* we are to approach God with our requests?
- What does David say in Psalm 143 that should motivate us to petition God?

- Based on this Psalm, for what things should we plead?
- Which verse from Psalm 143 would be helpful for you to memorize? Why?

Learning to Lament

A couple of Mark's prayers quoted in this faith lesson were prayers of lament. A lament is an honest, heartfelt expression of sorrow or grief. According to pastor and author Mark Vroegop, "Lament is how we bring our sorrow to God. Without lament, we won't know how to process pain. A lament reveals trust because, without hope in God's deliverance and the conviction that He's all-powerful, there would be no reason to lament when pain invades our lives."[21]

Resources

Here are two excellent, Bible-saturated books on prayers of lament. Both resources delve deeply into the psalms of lament.

1. Michael Card, *Sacred Sorrows: Reaching Out to God in The Lost Language of Lament* (NavPress, 2005).
2. Mark Vroegop, *Dark Clouds, Deep Mercy: Discovering The Grace of Lament* (Crossway, 2019).

Faith Lesson 3
EMBRACING BROKENNESS

"You and I will never meet God in revival until we first meet Him in brokenness." [22]

—Nancy DeMoss Wolgemuth

Approach the Word

Have you ever watched a Western TV show or movie in which a cowboy tries to ride a wild stallion?

Fenced in by a corral, the untamed horse—muscles rippling, snorting defiance—has never been ridden and he has no intention of cooperating. Time and again, the ranch hand jumps on the brute's back, only to be bucked. The cowboy's repeated efforts finally wear down the stallion and overcome the resistance. The horse succumbs to a saddle and rider and a bond develops between the two former foes.

Ranchers call this process "breaking a horse." Only by taming it, reducing it to submission, can they harness the potential of a wild stallion.[23]

Brokenness is also a means God employs that enables His servants to maximize their potential.

Just ask Mark Smith.

Absorb the Word

Mark emphatically claims, "I'm a broken man."

The external component of his remark is the brokenness of his physical body, which still pulsates with pain. Of even greater consequence is the internal component: a brokenness or poverty of spirit. For Mark, brokenness is a settled, permanent posture of the heart marked by absolute submission to God's will and mission, desperate dependence on His sustaining grace and tenderness toward others who hurt.

Mark cites David's reference to brokenness in Psalms 51:16–17: "Thou didst not delight in sacrifice, otherwise, I would give it; Thou are not pleased with burnt offering. The sacrifices of God are a broken spirit; a broken and a contrite heart, O God, Thou wilt not despise."

Though the cause of Mark's brokenness was an accident—not sin, as in David's case—the result was the same: a softer heart, a weaning from self-sufficiency and a recognition of need. Mark admits that even in ministry, success tends to instill arrogance. In his case, as Mark puts it, "brokenness helps prevent pride."

The process began in his hospital room right after the accident and initial surgery. "I couldn't function on my own," he concedes. "I couldn't lift a cup of water to my lips. I couldn't shift my body even an inch without crying out in pain. When I saw how helpless I was and how close I came to dying, I realized, 'I am nothing. I can't get a breath or live or ever serve God again without His power.'" That is when Mark says that he "developed less interest for my own reputation as a leader and a deeper yearning for God to be glorified in and through my life and ministry."

The muffling of pride isn't the only consequence of Mark's brokenness. Another is his willingness to be transparent.

You've read in his story that discouragement occasionally surfaced. When doctors took him off strong painkillers weeks after the accident, a full-blown episode of depression occurred. You've read his laments to the Lord, such as "Oh God, I can't take this anymore!" He divulges these inner symptoms of his accident because he doesn't mind if others see him as weak, so long as they see the Savior on whom he relies as strong.

His authenticity creates identification with and instills hope in people who hurt or struggle. They see Mark's pain and extraordinary usefulness and think, "Maybe God can use *me*, too."

Mark's softer heart toward God and others also makes him more sensitive to sin that crops up in his life. He sees his need spiritually, not just physically. Mark cites the prophet Isaiah's response after he saw a vision of God's majesty and holiness.

Isaiah cried, "Woe is me, for I am ruined! Because I am a man of unclean lips … for my eyes have seen the King, the Lord of hosts" (Isaiah 6:5).

A broken person is conscious of how he falls short and is quick to confess before God and man. Scottish writer George MacDonald commented on the importance of knowing our heart: "The only worse thing than being a sinner is not being aware of it."[24]

A single event may create an ongoing state of brokenness, but typical factors that create it include conviction and consequences of sin (as in David's case), chronic physical infirmity, temperamental weaknesses, failure or a long-lasting disappointment, such as a career that never panned out or estrangement from a loved one. "Trials make us bitter or better," Mark insists. When they wean us from self-reliance, instill a surrender to Christ's control and a desperation for His enablement, the result is a God-sanctioned mindset.

Though God puts a positive slant on brokenness, Satan counters with lies that discourage us from leadership or ministry engagement. He tries to convince us that a past mistake, chronic pain or emotional fragility that may come with a broken spirit disqualifies us from fruitful service. Yet Mark's story has vividly shown the opposite: *what some people perceive as a hindrance to our impact may be the pivot on which an influential life turns.*

If you're a broken person, be encouraged by Mark's story and by Alan Nelson's words about brokenness: "I doubt that people who have ever achieved significance, or who have been used productively by the Holy Spirit, have eluded this process."[25]

Key Truth

Even God-given success can instill pride and self-sufficiency. Some form of brokenness instills a more humble, God-honoring spirit. Brokenness may enhance one's ministry rather than hinder it.

Apply the Word

Read King Uzziah's story in 2 Chronicles 26. Use these questions to mine the passage.

- What evidences of a successful reign can you find?
- What words from the text explain the reasons for Uzziah's success?
- What evidence from the text indicates that Uzziah had *not* experienced brokenness?
- How did Uzziah's pride show?
- What were the consequences of his pride?

Link to Your Own Life

- How has the Lord blessed you, personally and professionally?
- In private prayers and through public testimony, have you given the Lord credit?
- Which of the positive outcomes of Mark's brokenness are true of you?
- If you have experienced something that has created a broken and contrite spirit within you—no matter how unpleasant it was—pause to thank the Lord for it right now.

Resources

1. *Embracing Brokenness,* by Alan Nelson (NavPress, 2002).

2. *Brokenness, Surrender, Holiness*, by Nancy DeMoss Wolgemuth (Moody Publishers, 2008).

3. *The Broken Way: A Daring Path into the Abundant Life,* by Ann Voskamp ((Zondervan, 2016).

Faith Lesson 4

RELEASING RESENTMENT

"Resentment is like drinking poison and hoping the other person dies." [26]

—St. Augustine of Hippo

Approach the Word

Has another person ever slandered you, besmirching your reputation with false accusations?

Has a business associate ever cheated you out of money and gotten away with it?

Has a loved one's betrayal sliced like shrapnel through your heart?

If you answer "Yes!" to one of these questions, you know how easily bitterness wells up inside and how difficult it is to forgive.

The driver who crossed the center line and rammed into Mark Smith's Taurus didn't do it intentionally or maliciously, yet his mistake cost the Smiths a lot of pain. In their story, they readily admitted the threat of resentment since their tribulation was no fault of their own.

When negative attitudes toward the other driver or toward God surfaced, how did they rein in the resentment, keeping it from enveloping them? What biblical principles did they apply that provided an antidote to the poison of bitterness that tried to infiltrate their bloodstream?

Absorb the Word

Initially, Debbie's resentment was prompted by observing Mark during physical therapy sessions. When she saw how much it hurt him, she focused on the unfairness of it all. "A few times I felt bitterness creeping in," she admits, "because all that Mark was going through was not his fault. When I heard him cry out, I'd start feeling anger and frustration toward God."

How did she deal with it?

"The Spirit would convict me each time and I'd confess it and cry out to Him for forgiveness, seeking His power to release any resentment." What she believed in her mind about God—His sovereignty and goodness—began seeping into her heart as well.

Sometimes Mark pondered, "Why did God allow this? Why did that driver cross the line?" He recognized that Satan wanted to take advantage of his vulnerable state to instill negative attitudes within him. "I kept rolling it over to God," Mark recalls. "I said to Him, 'God, in your strength, I forgive the other driver.'"

Mark's story revealed another strategy to prevent the buildup of bitterness. When he and Debbie prayed about whether to pursue a lawsuit against the other driver, God's Spirit didn't give them the freedom to proceed. Later, their Christian surgeon affirmed the decision. He believed that refusing to file a lawsuit accelerated Mark's healing and kept resentment at bay. Their decision freed Mark and Debbie to focus on the future, on getting better, rather than getting bogged down in legal processes that would have kept their thoughts on the past and the unfairness of their circumstance.

Christian maturity isn't demonstrated by the total absence of negative attitudes such as bitterness. We will not be totally like Christ until we see Him upon His return (1 John 3:2). What distinguishes a committed Christ-follower is how he or she *responds* to unfair circumstances, to mistreatment or to sin that the Holy Spirit exposes.

I am impressed by Mark's and Debbie's willingness to be transparent about what was going on inside them after the accident. By modeling how to handle the encroachment of bitterness, they lived victoriously and offer guidelines for us. To summarize, here are the steps they followed:

- As soon as God's Spirit convicted them of resentment, they confessed it. They were honest in dealing with their inappropriate attitude.
- They pleaded with the Lord for the strength to forgive the other driver. They chose, with God's help, to forgive him.
- They kept their focus on present recovery processes and a more favorable future, rather than choosing to rehash and concentrate on the unfairness of their predicament. With God's help, they refused to entertain thoughts that would spawn negativism.

Mark and Debbie were also aware of the most incisive verses in God's Word on the issue of forgiving others. "Let all bitterness and wrath and anger and clamor and slander be put away from you, along with malice. And be kind to one another, tender-hearted, forgiving each other, just as God in Christ also has forgiven you" (Ephesians 4:31–32).

This is a God-inspired command, which implies that *forgiving others is a choice!*

Why do Christians have the capacity to forgive someone who hurt us or whose actions caused us painful consequences? This verse suggests that *we've been forgiven far more!*

Key Truth

Releasing resentment is possible when we confess it, cry out to God for the strength to forgive and realize that our forgiveness of others is enabled by the forgiveness we have received from Christ.

Apply the Word

To personalize this faith lesson, think of an individual or group who has treated you unfairly or who has sinned against you. If there is one iota of resentment clinging to your heart, follow the steps modeled by Mark and Debbie as described in the preceding paragraphs.

Perhaps we think we've forgiven someone, yet beneath the surface of our hearts, barely detectable, resentment still simmers. To determine if you've really forgiven another, mull over the questions that follow. To derive the most benefit from these questions, turn them into a devotional time and examine the Bible reference(s) after each question.

A Word of Qualification: Forgiving someone does not always result in reconciliation of the relationship. Nor does our forgiveness relieve the other person of his or her responsibility before God. Nor does our act of forgiveness eradicate all consequences of the sin against us. The other person must cooperate with God for reconciliation to occur. When he or she doesn't, resting in the sovereignty of God concerning what happened to us is necessary in order to move on successfully.

Now ask the Holy Spirit to speak to you as you reflect on these questions:

- Have I done my part to seek reconciliation with this person? (Romans 12:18)
- Have thoughts of revenge or payback stopped surfacing in my mind? (Romans 12:19–21)

- Can I talk about this person without a hard edge to my tone of voice and without mean-spirited nonverbal communication? (Proverbs 15:1; Ephesians 4:31)
- Do I ever pray for this person and wish him or her well? (Matthew 5:44)
- Have I stopped telling others what this person did to me? (Ephesians 4:29)
- Am I willing to bless or to assist this person in a time of his or her need? (Exodus 23:4)
- Do I have more deep-seated joy than I previously experienced? Do I feel like a burden has been lifted off my shoulders? (Psalm 16:11)
- Do I walk more intimately with the Holy Spirit, sensing His presence and pleasure since He is no longer grieved by my bitterness? [27](Ephesians 4:30–32)

If you conclude that you have forgiven the perpetrator of your pain, thank the Lord right now for His enabling grace to do so. If your honest reflection indicates that resentment persists, follow Mark and Debbie's lead. Ask God for the capacity to do what you cannot do in your own strength: to forgive.

Resource

The best book I've read on dealing with resentment is R.T. Kendall's *Total Forgiveness: Revised and Updated* (Charisma House, 2007). Material in Chapter 2 of his book heavily influenced the reflective questions in this **Apply the Word** section.

Faith Lesson 5

USING MUSIC TO SOOTHE THE SOUL

"Music is medicine for the soul." [28]
—Marsha Hays

Approach the Word

T he catalyst of the Reformation, Martin Luther, knew the value of music in deepening faith and helping people focus on the character of God. He wrote, "Next to the Word of God, the noble art of music is the greatest treasure in the world. Music is one of the fairest and most glorious gifts of God, to which Satan is a bitter enemy, for it removes from the heart the weight of sorrow, and the fascination of evil thoughts."[29]

Mark and Debbie Smith experienced the value of music to refresh the spirit and inspire hope. During Mark's long recovery in 1996, songs became a means of God's grace to them.

Absorb the Word

In Chapter 5, Debbie admitted that on some days after Mark's accident, she felt so tired and emotionally numb caring for Mark and their son that she couldn't concentrate long enough to read the Bible in an unhurried fashion. That is when God's Spirit used a different means to comfort her. As she listened to Christian music, the Holy Spirit fed her soul through Bible texts that had been put to song.

While Mark recovered at home, he and Debbie often watched Gaither Homecoming videos. The songs enabled them to worship God, temporarily shifting their thoughts away from their circumstance to His character and promises. Despite his broken body, the lyrics to the hymn, "My Faith Has Found a Resting Place" comforted Mark's mind and heart.

God's Word teems with an emphasis on music.

An emphasis on worshipping God through music stitches together many pages of the Old Testament, especially in the Psalms. Typical of numerous verses is Psalm 104:33: "I will sing to the Lord as long as I live; I will sing praise to my God while I have my being." Tucked into a psalm prompted by persecution he experienced, David nonetheless wrote, "My lips will shout for joy when I sing praises to Thee" (Psalm 71:23).

During corporate worship services in the early church, songs offered not only praise to God, but mutual encouragement among the believers. Representative of several verses expressing this concept is Colossians 3:16: "Let the word of Christ richly dwell within you, with all wisdom teaching and admonishing one another with psalms and hymns and spiritual songs, singing with thankfulness in your hearts to God."

During a rough night in a Philippian jail, singing sustained Paul and Silas. They had been beaten with rods and their feet were fastened in the stocks. That is when they buoyed their spirits by "singing hymns of praise to God" (Acts 16:25).

A Christian blogger, Marsha Hays, echoes the Smiths' experience when it comes to the help of music during difficult times. In reference to words in Scripture that are put to music, she says, "Music that comes directly from the Word of God is medicine for the soul. God's words can bring healing, comfort, and encouragement like no other, but pairing those words with beautiful melodies implants them in my mind as well as my heart. The words get stuck in my mind, and throughout the day, in times of need, I sing the Scripture to myself."[30]

Dr. Michelle Bengtson, who wrote a highly regarded Christian book on depression, adds, "Listening to praise and worship music helped me to hold on when my grip was failing."[31] At the end of each chapter of *Hope Prevails* (2016), she provides a playlist of songs that ministered to her during her despondency.

My purpose is not to offer a comprehensive treatment of what the Bible says about music; rather, I want to extol its value for hurting people, whether the pain is physical or emotional. Even when our inner turmoil makes formulating a prayer difficult, hearing a song or our own singing offers a way to express faith and to sense God's presence during difficulty. Indeed, as Martin Luther attested, music is a great treasure for the Christian.

Key Truth

When God's people hurt, Christian music is a means of God's sustaining grace. What we hear or sing reminds us of who God is, what He has done and what He promises to do.

Apply the Word

Psalm 98:1–6 implores us to sing and offers reasons why. Read that passage slowly.

What reasons for singing to the Lord do these verses cite? (Look for what the psalmist implies, as well as what he directly states.)

For this psalmist, one thing that inspired singing was remembering past deeds of the Lord in relation to Israel. He had "done wonderful things" (vs.1). He had shown "faithfulness to the house of Israel" (vs.3).

Right now, perhaps you are hurting due to physical discomfort, the loss of a loved one or discouragement rooted in a circumstance you cannot control. To counter this pain, look over your shoulder and rekindle memories of God's past faithfulness to you, to your family, to your church, to your school or to your business. *How has He acted on your behalf in recent years?*

Find a song in your hymnbook or online that has buoyed your spirit at some point in the past whenever you sang or heard it. To find a song that comforts God's people during affliction, ask a music teacher or worship leader for titles.

Your choice may be a beloved hymn, such as "It Is Well with My Soul," or "Like A River Glorious." Perhaps it will be a contemporary song, such as "Through It All" or "Before the Throne of God Above." Or your selection may be a passage of God's Word put to music, such as "Oh God, You Are My God" (Psalm 63) or "Lord, From Sorrows Deep I Call" (Psalm 42). Listen to a recording of this song today or sing it yourself during your next quiet time. Employ it as a means of worshipping God, receiving comfort and as an impetus for thanking Him for His past interventions.

By praising Him in song for what He has already done, your faith for the current trial will be strengthened.

Faith Lesson 6

CULTIVATING FAITH BY REMEMBERING GOD'S PAST DEEDS

"True gratitude rests in the riches of God's grace as it looks back on the benefits it has received. By cherishing grace this way, it inclines the heart to trust in future grace. Gratitude exults in the past benefits of God and says to faith, 'Embrace more of these benefits, so that looking back on God's deliverance may continue.'"[32]

—John Piper

Approach the Word

What threatens the vitality of your faith in the Lord?

Does your capacity to trust Him totter when bills pile up due to unemployment? Do you vacillate between trust and doubt when there is conflict at work or when you are grieving over estrangement from a loved one? Does a depressive episode test your faith in Christ, or is your faith challenged by debilitating physical pain that keeps throbbing no matter how many meds you swallow? Is your organization or company facing what looks like an insurmountable hurdle to stay financially solvent or to reach growth goals?

Perhaps the more important question is this:

What instills the faith that you need to face these kind of setbacks or obstacles?

One of the answers to this question is application of a clear biblical principle that, on multiple occasions, has boosted Mark Smith's faith in the Lord.

Absorb the Word

As a Christian university president, Mark often envisions new programs and facilities that will enhance fulfillment of the school's mission. Then his vision requires resources. What gives him bold faith to believe that God will provide through the donors with whom he speaks? What has fueled the trust in the Lord that has enabled him to raise huge amounts for Christian schools?

What strengthens the faith he needs to keep throbbing pain from sabotaging a workday's responsibilities?

What Mark Learned from His Past

A faith-strengthening practice he relies on is *remembering God's past faithfulness*. When he looks over his shoulder and remembers past answers to prayer, his faith for a personal or university need is cultivated. He faces obstacles optimistically and thinks, "*Do it again, Lord!*"

"In 1996, I saw how God answered desperate prayers offered from my hospital bed," Mark recalls. "He met our financial needs, answered my plea for sleep and an end to nightmares about the crash, and promoted healing of my body to a far greater extent than doctors expected. That prompted me to trust Him more and more as the years went by. The accident and its aftermath made me a man of prayer and faith."

Remembering God's past faithfulness—even answers to prayer prior to the accident, as disclosed in Chapter 2 of Mark's story—sustains Mark and Debbie through current trials and prompts Mark to make bold requests on behalf of the university he serves.

"I keep expecting God to do more because of what I have seen Him do in the past," Mark explains. "My faith increased incrementally, as I kept accumulating memories of His past faithfulness."

Even when Mark is hurting physically, one reason he perseveres is awareness of all the times God enabled him to keep going in the past.

Biblical Basis for the Principle

Remembering God's past deeds is a theme that surfaces in many parts of Scripture. God wanted His chosen people to remember His past miracles and provision. He often referred to Himself as "*I am the God who...*," then He'd recite a specific incident, such as bringing them out of Egypt or into the land of Canaan (Deuteronomy 5:6; Leviticus 25:38). When they forgot His past works, He grieved. The psalmist even equated such forgetfulness with rebellion: "They did not remember Your abundant kindnesses, but rebelled by the sea… They forgot God their Savior, who had done great things in Egypt" (Psalm 106:7, 21).

The Old Testament even commands a recollection of God's deeds. "Remember His wonders which He has done" (Psalm 105:5), and "Give heed to yourself lest you forget the things which your eyes have seen" (Deuteronomy 4:9).

Of special interest in this faith lesson is the correlation between remembering and faith. After pointing out how their forgetfulness of His past deeds hurt God, the author of Psalm 78 linked forgetfulness and unbelief. "They did not believe in God, and did not trust in His salvation" (Psalm 78:22).

Jesus also linked remembering His past deeds to trusting Him for current needs. Mark 8:13–21 records a story involving Jesus in a conversation with His disciples while they were in a boat. His followers were complaining about their lack of bread. This conversation occurred subsequent to Jesus' feeding of 4,000 persons with seven loaves of bread and a few small fish (Mark 8:5–7).

Jesus reminded them of *two* recent incidences when He had fed a multitude with a minimal amount of food. When they had correctly answered His factual review questions about those miracles, Jesus lamented, "Do you not yet understand?" (vs.21).

What was Jesus' teaching point? He was saying that His past performance which they had observed should have buttressed their faith in relation to the present need for bread. They failed to "put the past into the present tense" by realizing that the ultimate provider was in the boat with them!

As He reviewed the previous miracles, Jesus asked His disciples, *"Do you remember when I...?"* Then He recited, in specific terms, what He had done for the crowds.

When we face peace-robbing situations or needs that exceed our ability to meet, He whispers the same question to us: *"Terry* (or *Susan* or *Bob*), *do you remember when I...?"*

He wants us to reply with a resounding "Yes!" He yearns for us to plead, *"Do it again, Lord!"*

Key Truth

Recalling the Lord's past performance on our behalf sustains us during present difficulty and engenders within us the faith to persevere.

Apply the Word

Identify a few specific ways God has intervened for you in the past: answers to prayer, unexpected provision for needs or resolution of problems.

How should your recollection of the Lord's past faithfulness affect your response to any current trial or challenge you are facing? Thank Him for the past incidences of His faithfulness. Ask Him to use those memories to deepen your faith for handling a current crisis or stressor.

For parents or grandparents. The memories that boost your faith can exert the same effect on the faith of your young children or grandkids. The commands couched in Psalm 145 apply to all believers, yet have special pertinence to you. Read this psalm. Then zero in on God's desired response on our part to His past deeds.

In addition to gratitude, God tells us through David to "declare Thy mighty acts" (vs.4); to "speak of the power of Thine awesome acts" (vs.6); to "eagerly utter the memory of Thine abundant goodness" (vs.7) and to "make known to the sons of men Thy mighty acts" (vs.12).

This call to share memories of His faithfulness is especially applicable to parents and grandparents due to verse 4: "One generation shall praise Thy works to another."

While you are driving with the kids, tucking them in at night or involved in a formal family devotional time, make it a habit to tell interesting stories of how God intervened for you in the past. If your child or grandchild was old enough at the time of God's intervention, start your story with *"Remember when…?"* Even if the incident occurred before they were born, fill their minds with stories that depict our Lord as a caring provider.

The next time you have such an opportunity, what story will you share with your son, daughter or grandchild?

Resources

Here are two excellent books on expressing gratitude to God for things He has done for us.

1. Nancy Leigh DeMoss, *Choosing Gratitude: Your Journey to Joy* (Moody Publishers, 2009).
2. Ann Voskamp, *One Thousand Gifts* (Zondervan, 2010).

Faith Lesson 7

MODELING THE MESSAGE

"A message prepared in a mind will reach a mind. A message prepared in a life will reach a life."[33]

—Bill Gothard

Approach the Word

If you aren't a pastor, put yourself in the shoes of one as you read this predicament.

As you prepare and deliver a series of sermons on faith, you ask the Lord to deepen your own capacity to trust Him. You deliver the messages: defining faith, explaining how it is a prerequisite for pleasing God and illustrating factors that fuel its growth.

Then the week after your series ends, an unexpected housing expense demolishes your personal budget. Someone in the church starts a rumor about you that is blatantly false. A call from your daughter hints that an unbelieving college roommate is negatively influencing her.

What is going on? Why are these threats occurring *now*, back to back to back? Is there a perspective that could change how you view these unsettling circumstances and better prepare you to respond wisely to them?

Yes.

This chapter will explain that perspective and fit you with new lenses so you can clearly see a vital principle that is especially pertinent to persons who communicate Scripture, whether in vocational ministry or lay settings.

Absorb the Word

If you regularly communicate God's Word in any form or venue—preaching, classroom teaching, blogging or personal witnessing—a principle sprouting from the soil of Mark's story is especially pertinent to you. First, let's review the background for that principle.

On March 3, 1996, right before his serious auto crash, Mark spoke in a church on 2 Corinthians 12:9–10. When Paul asked God three times to remove a thorn in the flesh, the Lord said "No." God assured Paul, "My grace is sufficient for you." Then Paul's perspective changed and he accepted his limitations and difficulties. He asserted, "When I am weak, then I am strong."

That morning, Mark put his sermon spotlight on this truth: *God's grace is sufficient for any situation that we face.* A couple of hours later, he would begin a lifelong pilgrimage that would provide a daily opportunity to apply his own sermon.

What is the principle that is so vital to communicators? Allow me to give you an amplified version of it: *God yearns for His messengers to embody what they communicate, to live out and to experience the truths they explain to others. He often puts His spokespersons in situations that test them on the material they convey or which provide a rich opportunity to apply it. The ultimate outcome God seeks is a communicator with ever-increasing authenticity, whose message resonates with people because it was prepared in a life, not just in his or her mind.*

In the introduction to this faith lesson, the pastor who taught on faith faced multiple threats that required him to exercise faith.

Prior to the accident, Mark Smith already served as a positive role model of faith and he was no stranger to the grace of God about which he spoke. However, in God's mysterious providence, He wanted Mark to experience an even deeper grasp of His all-sufficient grace, which would positively shape the remainder of his life and ministry.

In order to instill this principle into His servants, God doesn't routinely allow or design a circumstance as grievous as what Mark experienced. Mark's life-changing accident and the lingering pain are parts of God's challenging "divine curriculum" for him and his wife, Debbie, in order to prepare them for a future of extraordinary leadership effectiveness. Like Paul, Mark's frailty resulting from the accident ensures that his success does not breed conceit and instills a daily dependence on the Lord for effectiveness.

God wants preachers, teachers, writers and witnesses to prepare their material in their lives, not just in their minds. He wants passion for doctrine to stem from an experience of it, not just from their cognitive ability to exegete a text. He desires credibility on the topic that draws audiences to His messengers like iron shavings to a magnet. Who a communicator *is* radically affects the power of what he or she *says*.

Mark's accident and its aftermath provide an extraordinary example of this principle. I asked him to give me other, less dramatic examples of God's desire to build the message even deeper into His messengers. "I gave a series of messages on family relationships," Mark replied. "During that series, issues surfaced in our home that offered more than the usual opportunities to apply the relational insights I was preaching. Similarly, I remember what happened after I gave a message on patience. Within days, I faced unexpected personal and ministry circumstances that required a double portion of patience.

"On a more positive note, I often speak on the importance of personal evangelism. When I do, within a few days the Lord provides unexpected, spontaneous opportunities for me to share my testimony and the gospel. Either right before or subsequent to speaking on personal witnessing, I have learned to be alert to these unexpected opportunities. God wants to see if I'll do what I tell others to do."

A well-known pastor and author, Warren Wiersbe, wrote a book on spiritual warfare which included ways to refute Satan's attempts to derail us. Wiersbe divulged that as he wrote it, he faced an escalation of spiritual opposition and temptation to sin.[34] Since Satan cannot touch God's people without God the Father's permission (Job 1: 8–12; Luke 22:31–32), even Satan's attempts to harm us may be, in disguise, a way in which the Lord tries to embed such a message deeper into our hearts.

Key Truth

When we communicate His Word in any form or venue, God desires to plant the message into us so we model it, rather than just speak on it. He designs opportunities for us to practice what we communicate or to grow in relation to the subject matter we convey so our message increases in authenticity and effectiveness.

Apply the Word

What are logical applications of this principle for communicators?

Pray proactively. As you prepare for a sermon or work on the draft of a blog or book chapter, invite the Lord to help you live out the message, not just deliver it, so you share it more passionately and practically. Ask the Holy Spirit to sharpen your sensitivity so you won't overlook an opportunity to apply what you're communicating.

Stay alert. Ask God for discernment, so when negative circumstances converge or stress ramps up in relationships, you will know when it is a divine opportunity to pass a test on something you have taught or written recently. Anticipating a test of what you've taught (or will soon teach) increases your chances of passing it.

Mark mentioned that he tries to stay alert to ways in which God wants to work in him in relation to a message he gives. The example he cited dealt with unplanned opportunities for personal evangelism, preceding or shortly after speaking on the subject. Examine these verses on the necessity of staying alert as a Christian:

"Be on the alert, stand firm in the faith, act like men, be strong" (1 Corinthians 16:13).

In a context dealing with the second coming of Christ, Paul wrote, "So then let us not sleep as others do, but let us be alert and sober" (1 Thessalonians 5:6).

- When the Lord wants to test us on a message or provide an application opportunity, how does staying alert or watchful help us cooperate better with Him?
- What topic, truth or Bible passage will you be sharing with others in the near future? If you stay alert and watchful in relation to this content, in what ways might God try to test you on it? What potential opportunities for personal application can you spot on the horizon?

Anticipate the enemy's attack. Mull over this question: How is Satan likely to thwart my efforts to apply what I communicate? Knowing your own areas of vulnerability, as well as your history in relation to the enemy, enhance your capacity to answer that question. Then claim this promise from 2 Thessalonians 3:3: "The Lord is faithful, and He will strengthen and protect you from the evil one."

Insert personal anecdotes into your messages or writing. Employ stories that show how the truths you convey have challenged or comforted you. When has your own recall of the Bible verses and truths helped carry you through a burdensome time? Discreet transparency creates identification with your audience and glorifies God by putting the spotlight on His enablement of you during a time of difficulty.

On March 3, 1996, Mark spoke clearly and accurately on God's sustaining grace. For the past 24 years, his daily dependence on the Lord has proclaimed the same message more convincingly than ever.

Faith Lesson 8

DISCERNING GOD'S CALL TO MINISTRY

What ministry burden has God given to you? What piece of God's heart for the church, community or world do you carry? What have you done for the Lord that left you with the impression, "Yes—God made me for this!"?

This is a faith lesson for young adults or adolescents who may wonder if God is calling them to vocational ministry, or for parents/youth leaders who love them or work with them.

Approach the Word

Leslie, a high school senior, feels an inner tug to become a youth worker in a local church or parachurch organization. She wants to exert the same kind of positive influence on kids that her youth pastor has had on her. She realizes that pursuing this direction would mean changing her college plans. "How can I be sure God is calling me to this?" she asks herself.

Their local church's missions conference sparked Ted and Susan's interest in overseas ministry. Now when they pray together, their intercessions include missionaries supported by their church. They've also pledged more of their money to missions.

They've wondered aloud, "Is the Lord calling us to serve as missionaries?" Ted and Susan are open to the idea, but know it would involve major adjustments and challenges. They want to be sure it's the Lord who is prompting them, not their own initiative.

Randy leads an adult Bible study class. He receives lots of positive feedback on his teaching. He loves to dig into God's Word for himself as he prepares.

Subtly, Randy senses God may be calling him to be a pastor. He wonders if there is a link between a waning enthusiasm for his job and the inner longing to teach God's Word more often. He and his wife are discussing the implications of such a drastic vocational shift. What else can they do to confirm this sense of call?

How can individuals or couples know when God is calling them to pursue a vocational ministry? What steps can they take to determine if God is leading them?

In Chapter 2 of Mark's story, you read about his calling as a teen to serve the Lord vocationally. In the decades since then, he has accumulated wisdom to help teens and younger adults think through the question of God's call. You'll discover his insights and more in this faith lesson.

Absorb the Word

I'll lay the groundwork for Mark's counsel on a ministry call with three vital insights.

Perspectives on Calling

In the New Testament, verses that mention God's "call" typically refer to conversion. God prepares the hearts of individuals who put their faith in Christ and His sacrificial death for their sin.

When Paul told members of the church at Corinth to "Consider your calling…" (1 Corinthians 1:26), he was referring to the time they put their faith in Christ for salvation. Ephesians 4:1 uses "calling" in the same sense. He told church members "to walk in a manner worthy of the calling with which you have been called."

This biblical use of the concept of calling does *not* preclude a separate, special calling to some sphere of vocational ministry. In most instances, one's call to salvation and a call to vocational ministry are separated by time.

In a general sense, God calls all Christians to minister in some form. He has distributed to every believer at least one spiritual gift or capacity for service (1 Corinthians 12:7). Every believer has a role to play as a "minister of reconciliation" and as an "ambassador for Christ" (2 Corinthians 5:18–20). A part of a pastor's job description is to equip church members so *they* engage in "the work of service" (Ephesians 4:11–12).

What a privilege every Christian has to participate in God's redemptive work! *A non-ministering Christian is the ultimate oxymoron.*

God calls many persons to serve in the marketplace. He gives them the abilities and instills the passion for them to work in the business world, in medical professions, in financial management, in the political realm and in other venues. In such arenas, His people serve as salt and light (Matthew 5:13–16), offering a testimony of faith and modeling biblical values in places where vocational Christian workers often do not exert a strong influence.

Perhaps the best historical example of a "marketplace calling" was William Wilberforce (1759–1833). Despite heavy opposition and the loss of friendships, he labored for decades to end the slave trade, then slave ownership, in Great Britain. He persevered because he knew God had called him to serve in Parliament for this purpose.

But God also summons some of His people to some type of vocational Christian ministry. Let's shift to Mark's pointers for discerning such a calling.

Pointers About Calling

I've taken Mark's counsel pertaining to a call to vocational ministry and put his tips in the form of questions. There's no escaping the fact that such a call is a subjective thing, yet the following ideas may increase one's objectivity.

Am I making this decision in the context of a vibrant, daily walk with Christ? Mark advocates earnest prayer and delving into Scripture to seek God's wisdom on the matter. He puts these means of grace in a larger framework. According to Mark, "A person who prays *consistently* and who *regularly* feeds on God's Word is in a better position to hear the Holy Spirit when He speaks about his or her future."

Seeking God only when there's a major decision to make usually doesn't instill the wisdom or sensitivity needed to hear Him clearly. It's the *habit* of prayer and Bible reading that helps one determine when the Spirit is speaking or whether false motivations are vying for control.

Do I have a compelling desire to serve the Lord? "God doesn't usually force someone into a ministry," Mark says. "A passion for or attraction to a ministry typically accompanies His summons."

Has God given me the necessary gifts and abilities to succeed in ministry? Answering this question is easier when one has been serving as a volunteer within his or her local church. Certain spiritual gifts—especially those involving skills, such as teaching or leadership—emerge through activity. If God calls a person to preach, the teaching gift will typically surface when teaching a Sunday School class or leading a small group Bible study. A leadership or administrative gift may show when one leads a task force or helps plan a retreat. This is a question that is difficult to answer in a vacuum, without hands-on experience in volunteer venues.

Do I sense a strong, inner confirmation of the Holy Spirit for this calling? "Yes, this is a subjective element," Mark admits, "but such a resolute conviction needs to be present."

Mark's next guideline balances the subjectivity of his previous one.

Have other Christians confirmed my calling and the gifts it will require? Those who know the character of the person, who have observed this person's various volunteer ministries, are in a good position to affirm or to question a call to serve vocationally. "The confirmation of the saints is a critical component of one's decision," Mark asserts.

As a teen, not long after he sensed God leading him to vocational service, Mark announced his change of plans in front of his local congregation. If leaders of his church had questioned his calling or his fitness for it, they wouldn't have given him a public venue to announce it.

Are you willing to prepare for the ministry to which you feel called?

For example, to assume the role of a pastor or missionary usually requires a formal education in Bible, plus intense training in the skill-set and tasks germane to a particular position.

Key Truth

Though God calls all Christians to serve Him, to some individuals He extends an invitation to minister full time in a sphere of vocational service. Experienced, godly leaders can provide the counsel necessary to persons considering such a calling.

Apply the Word

If you feel God may be nudging you into vocational ministry, go back and review the six questions Mark posed earlier in this faith lesson. Can you say "Yes" to all six questions? If not, what steps can you take now to make a "Yes" possible in the future?

Pay special attention to the question about your church's confirmation. Perhaps someone has complimented you for your teaching, for your leadership of a task force, for your planning of a retreat or for your personal evangelism. Now take it a step further.

If your senior pastor knows you well, seek his feedback. If your pastor is new, ask him if there is a procedure in place for you to seek confirmation from the church's official board or governing body. According to Proverbs 11:14, "Where there is no guidance, the people fall, but in abundance of counselors there is victory."

Keep praying diligently for the Lord's wisdom. He promises to supply it! "If any of you lacks wisdom, let him ask of God, who gives to all men generously and without reproach, and it will be given to him" (James 1:5).

Could your future include Columbia International University?

Whether you think God is calling you to vocational ministry or to the marketplace, consider the excellent educational opportunities at Columbia International University. Even if you don't know your career plans before enrolling, that is okay. Many persons in your stage of life just know they want a biblical education in an environment governed by Christian values. Students often discover God's career call on their lives during their years at a Christian college.

Contact Information

Columbia International University
7435 Monticello Road
Columbia, SC 29203
Phone 803.754.4100 or 800.777.2227

COMFORTING PERSONS WHO HURT

"God never teaches us or comforts us solely for our own benefit." [35]

—Stuart Briscoe

Approach the Word

While strolling alone on a beach near his home, the forlorn pastor considered suicide. He thought to himself, "I can't take any more hard knocks. I can't imagine how things will get any better."

A worried friend of the pastor showed up at the beach. The friend didn't condemn his depressed companion for lack of faith or dish out superficial solutions. Instead, he walked alongside him for a long time, listened as the pastor vented, told him he loved him and prayed for him.

The friend's presence incarnated God's love and instilled hope within the distraught pastor. Here's how the pastor described the effect: "Within minutes, my life started coming together again. I started thinking clearly for a change. A ray of hope burst through the dark clouds that had been hovering over me. I began seeing solutions to some of the things harassing me and believed again that God would help me."

What prompted the compassionate response of the pastor's friend?

His own past experience with pain.

The comforter had gone through a rough patch in his life a couple of years before. He knew firsthand how downcast a person could feel and had experienced the sustaining power of God's Spirit. He remembered how God had mobilized people in the body of Christ to reach out to him. The comforter's own brokenness had kept him from a self-righteous, judgmental attitude toward his pastor friend. Instead of offering glib, snap-out-of-it advice, his listening posture and heartfelt prayer had lifted the rocks off his friend's chest.

Similarly, Mark and Debbie Smith received soul-strengthening ministry from others in the family of God. As a result, their own sensitivity to others who hurt escalated. Like the pastor's comforter, their pain expanded their ministry to others.

Absorb the Word

For Debbie, one effect of Mark's accident and its aftermath is an enhanced ministry of intercession. "I now take prayer requests more seriously," she asserts. "We relied on others' prayers so much and now I'm more prone to pray when I hear or read a request, rather than take it for granted."

Over time, especially owing to his ongoing pain stemming from the accident, Mark's pastoral heart has enlarged to complement his driven, goal-oriented leadership traits. As one colleague put it, "Mark has a tender heart. He cares about people and persons who hurt are drawn to him because of it."

In his story, you read how his heart for people exhibited itself through winsome personal evangelism, through provision of educational opportunities for the underprivileged, through community revitalization in neighborhoods close to the schools he has served and through his Sunday morning prayer tweets for pastors—along with the Pastor's Retreat Center he started. His vision for huge educational initiatives and program enhancements doesn't obscure his capacity to see the needs of individuals.

Mark's broken body has softened his heart, resulting in an expanded ministry of encouragement and comfort in relation to others. Like the pastor's friend in the introduction to this faith lesson, his experience of God's grace during pain means he has more grace to offer others.

A biblical basis for this theme is 2 Corinthians 1:3–11. One outcome Paul cited for receiving God's comfort during the suffering that he and his team faced was "so that we may be able to comfort those who are in any affliction with the comfort with which we ourselves are comforted by God" (vs.4). Paul went on to say, "If we are afflicted, it is for your comfort…or if we are comforted, it is for your comfort" (vs.6).

This text discloses a second outcome of Paul's persecution: a weaning from self-reliance, leading to a greater dependence on God (vs.8–9). Yet his suffering, along with the divine help he received, also had the horizontal effect of expanding his ministry of comfort.

Paul's inspired words and the Smiths' experience reveal four reasons why sufferers make the best comforters:

1. They know what it is like to hurt grievously.
2. They receive some form of God's comfort, whether from His Word, through prayer or through others in the body of Christ.
3. Their own brokenness softens their heart toward others who suffer.
4. Those who hurt are more receptive to the help offered by individuals who can identify with their pain.

Key Truth

One potential outcome of suffering is an increased capacity to comfort others going through difficulty. Our adversity provides an opportunity to receive God's comfort, which, in turn, enhances our sensitivity to hurting people.

Apply the Word

What are logical responses to this faith lesson?

Effect on Your Prayers

Whether your suffering is physical, emotional or circumstantial, you have every right as God's child to plead for Him to alleviate the pain or to resolve the worrisome dilemma. Psalm 55:22 represents many Bible verses that invite us to approach Him with our needs: "Cast your burden upon the Lord, and He will sustain you."

Consider adding a new prayer as well. Use words similar to the following: "*Lord, please don't waste this pain. Use it to increase my compassion for others who hurt so I can pass along the grace I've received from You and from others. In the name of One who suffered not for Himself, but for others. Amen.*"

Effect on What You Share with People

Think of one problem or form of suffering you have experienced in recent years. Perhaps it is a trial you are still going through. Then mull over these questions in an unhurried fashion.

- As an outcome of this pain, how has the Lord become more real and personal to you?
- How did He intervene or act to assist you?
- How did He employ others in the body of Christ to minister to you during the ordeal?
- What did you learn from the painful experience, spiritually speaking?
- How did it deepen or solidify your faith in the Lord?

Allow your answers to those questions to become content for some form of personal testimony.

If you're a member of a small group or Sunday School class, ask for a few minutes to share your story and how you experienced God's grace in the midst of your pain. If you teach or preach, when it is relevant to the Bible passage or topic you are covering, share your story as an illustration of God's sustenance or intervention. If you meet with a person who's hurting—like the pastor's friend on the beach—allow your own experience to make you a better listener and intercessor on the person's behalf. *After* you listen well, if you believe your story will extend hope to this hurting person, share it gently and warmly.

Every time the Lord comforts you, ask Him for opportunities to give away what you've received.

Faith Lesson 10

REDEEMING PAIN

"God sees our lowest moments as our spiritual highs because that is when He is doing the deepest work in us. And it is out of those valleys that God gives us our platform for ministry." [36]

—Vaneetha Risner

"One of the things held out to grieving or suffering believers is the prospect of being more fruitful than they could have ever imagined." [37]

—D.A. Carson

Approach the Word

What happened seemed nonsensical.

Why did a 30-year-old man with fervent faith in Christ, who had received a clear-cut call from God to Christian college administration, experience a near-fatal car accident that was not his fault, within three months of starting his first college administrative position?

He had a horrific accident that entailed weeks of utter physical helplessness, searing pain, months of arduous physical therapy to learn how to walk again and medical bills that far exceeded insurance coverage. His calamity has generated acute pain every day of the 24-plus years since it occurred.

Scripture suggests that what does not make sense to us makes perfect sense to a sovereign God. God has "made foolish the wisdom of the world" (1 Corinthians 1:20). "The foolishness of God is wiser than men" (1 Corinthians 1:25). Through Isaiah, God declared, "My thoughts are not your thoughts, neither are your ways My ways … for as the heavens are higher than the earth, so are My ways higher than your ways" (Isaiah 55:8–9).

God has a way of redeeming pain, of gleaning positive outcomes from deep suffering.

The verb "to redeem" carries special significance to Christians. Jesus redeemed us from the penalty of sin, paying the ransom of His life to free us from the control of Satan and the eternal consequences of sin. In broad terms, to redeem means to exchange one thing for another, such as redeeming a coupon so you can receive a discounted price. It suggests receiving a benefit, to recoup something feared lost.

Since God is in control, our pain can serve a redemptive purpose far more significant than our earthly comfort.

What positive outcomes of pain does God's Word cite? How has Mark Smith and others quoted in this faith lesson observed divine wisdom behind God's dark providence?

Absorb the Word

Selectivity of Content

The library shelves of Christian colleges and seminaries sag with the weight of pastoral and theological tomes on the issues pertaining to suffering and faith. In the next few pages, I realize I'm only scratching the surface of a complex and mysterious topic. What follows is by necessity highly selective. To delve deeper into the subject of pain, see the **Resources** section in the back of this book for a few choice titles that offer a blend of raw personal story and sound biblical perspectives.

Potential Benefits of Pain

Any type of pain can increase our intimacy with the Lord. When affliction renders us needy and helpless, we have no other recourse but to pray regularly for the strength to endure, and if physically able, for the resiliency to keep serving and fulfilling our responsibilities. The constant communication with our Savior enhances our fellowship with Him and heightens our awareness of His moment-by-moment presence.

Mark's primary means of handling daily physical pain are prayers for strength interspersed throughout his day.

Experiencing the Lord's hour-by-hour sustenance has increased His love and appreciation for His Savior. Of course, Mark loved Him before the accident, but ever since, his enjoyment of the Lord's presence has escalated.

Charles Spurgeon, a nineteenth century British pastor, experienced two sources of recurring pain: depression and severe gout. Zack Eswine, his biographer, concluded, "The presence of God during his pain became more blessed to him than the absence of pain."[38] Elisabeth Elliot, who lost two husbands early in her life, said, "Through my own troubles, God has not given me explanations. But He has met me as a person, as an individual, and that's what we most need."[39]

Joni Eareckson Tada, who has been a quadriplegic since a diving accident in her teens, wrote, "Somehow, in the midst of your suffering, the Son of God beckons you into the inner sanctum of His own suffering—a place of mystery and privilege. I have suffered, yes. But I wouldn't trade places with anybody in the world to be this close to Jesus."[40]

Experiencing God's grace during trouble deepens our faith in Him. Whether the Lord's intervention alters our threatening circumstance or merely strengthens us within so we can better bear it, His help deepens our capacity to trust Him in the future. Referring to a burdensome situation he experienced in Asia, Paul wrote, "We had the sentence of death within ourselves in order that we should not trust in ourselves, but in God who raises the dead" (2 Corinthians 1:9).

The Lord doesn't deepen our faith so much through a lecture or by reading a book as He does by putting us in a situation in which reliance on Him is the only viable option.

In Mark's story, you read how his capacity to trust the Lord for personal needs, as well as for the challenges faced by the schools he has led, grew incrementally over time. Seeing the Lord answer desperate prayers from his hospital bed strengthened his faith enough to ask God for challenging financial needs of the schools. Experiencing God's recurring answers to prayer prompted Mark to make what I call "bigger and bigger asks" of God for the sake of accomplishing Kingdom business. "The accident made me a man of prayer and faith," Mark concludes.

According to James I. Packer, God strives to "overwhelm us with a sense of our own inadequacy and to drive us to cling to Him more closely. He fills our lives with troubles and perplexities to ensure that we learn to hold Him fast. He takes steps to drive us out of self-confidence to trust in Himself."[41]

"Therefore we do not lose heart, but though our outer man is decaying, yet our inner man is being renewed day by day. For momentary, light affliction is producing for us an eternal weight of glory far beyond all comparison" (2 Corinthians 4:16–17).

Pain purifies and deepens our character. The Apostle Paul testified that he exulted in his tribulations. Why? "Tribulation brings about perseverance; and perseverance, proven character; and proven character, hope" (Romans 5:3–4). James echoed Paul's sentiment: "The testing of your faith produces endurance.

And let endurance have its perfect result, that you may be perfect and complete, lacking in nothing" (James 1:2–4).

Mark admits that much of his early ministry was "more about me and what I could accomplish than it should have been." Desperate dependence on the Lord spawned by his accident instilled a realization that ministry was all about the Lord's glory, not his own. The result was a less self-centered, more humble spirit.

The effect on his character has probably been more preventive in nature. He says, "Without the pain caused by the accident, the success I've had in personal and corporate ministry could have birthed pride, a trait which typically causes a domino effect and further erodes one's character."

Pain packs the potential to expand our ministry impact. Mark's awareness of life's fragility has instilled an intense urgency for personal evangelism, preaching and aggressive program initiatives at schools to expand the training of future leaders. His capacity to trust God for the funds needed to implement his vision was enlarged by how God answered his prayers while in a state of helplessness after the accident. Mark adamantly claims, "The accident made me the leader I am today."

Scripture teems with examples of how God redeems pain for a redemptive purpose, but I'll cite only two.

Joseph's brothers sold him into slavery. Years later, he interpreted the Pharaoh's dream, which forecasted seven years of abundance followed by seven years of famine for Egypt and surrounding areas. When he was promoted to a ruling position, Joseph devised a plan for preserving produce and grain so there would be food during the long famine. When he met his brothers years later, he told them, "You meant evil against me, but God meant it for good in order to bring about this present result, to preserve many people alive" (Genesis 50:20).

It appeared that the imprisonment of Paul would curtail the spread of the gospel. Instead, the opposite happened. When other believers heard of Paul's confinement, they began taking his place, speaking boldly of Christ. Here's how Paul summed up the effect of his affliction: "My circumstances have turned out for the greater progress of the gospel" (Philippians 1:12).

For a contemporary example, since her paralysis Joni Eareckson Tada has written best-selling books extolling the gospel and has given her testimony of deep faith in Christ all over the world. She established *Joni and Friends,* an organization that provides support and resources for disabled persons and their caregivers. Her impact for the gospel isn't huge *in spite of* her accident, but *because* of it. Her own words offer an apt summary of ways in which the Lord redeems pain. Her prayer alludes to God's refusal to heal her body.

"Thank You for the deeper healing You gave me. That *no* meant *yes* to a stronger faith in You, a deeper prayer life, and a greater understanding of Your Word. It has purged sin from my life, forced me to depend on Your grace, and increased my compassion for others who hurt. It has stirred an excitement about heaven, and pushed me to give thanks in times of sorrow. It has helped me to love You more, Jesus."[42]

She went on to say, "He didn't give me the physical healing I had wanted, but the deeper healing I needed so much more."

A Realistic Perspective

I'd be remiss if I didn't acknowledge an inescapable fact: not every Christian who suffers deeply sees an observable reason *why.* God has reasons that we might not grasp in this life. When we cannot see a *why,* our only recourse is to trust in a *Who*: a personal God who suffered Himself by sacrificing His only Son on a cross, who asks us to trust Him even when we don't understand, when His dark providence hurts. Even when we cannot identify a reason for our pain, we know two things:

God pledges to be with us when we hurt and to sustain us through the pain. King David declared, "The Lord is near to the brokenhearted, and saves those who are crushed in spirit" (Psalm 34:18). Another Psalmist added, "He heals the brokenhearted, and binds up their wounds" (Psalm 147:3).

The pain and suffering experienced by God's children are temporary. In the new heaven and new earth, "He shall wipe away every tear from their eyes; and there shall no longer be any death; there shall no longer be any mourning, or crying, or pain" (Revelation 21:4). This assurance is the key to resiliency during suffering. Paul referred to Jesus' resurrection—and ours—as the reason he could say in the midst of suffering, "Therefore, we do not lose heart" (2 Corinthians 4:14–18).

Key Truth

Suffering in a Christian serves a redemptive purpose. Potential benefits include greater intimacy with Christ, deeper faith in Him, the purifying of our character and an expanded ministry impact.

Apply the Word

- In your own life, how have you experienced a spiritual or ministry benefit as a result of an affliction or setback? Pause and thank God right now for how He has redeemed your pain.

- How have you observed a positive outcome of suffering in the life of another person? To encourage this person, write a note explaining how you've seen God work in and through him or her.

- Which Bible verse woven into this faith lesson speaks loudest to you right now? Why?

- Within this faith lesson, which quote from an outside source resonates most with you? Why?

The next time you are hurting, it's appropriate to ask God for total healing, or for Him to remove the fearful circumstance or to strengthen your spirit so you can bear it gracefully. But also ask Him to use your pain for your long-term spiritual good and for expansion of your borders of influence for Him, even if you don't see it happen during your earthly pilgrimage.

Make this your prayer:

"Father, I'd rather not have this pain, but for now, You've given it to me. Do what is best for me spiritually and what will give most glory to You. Please don't waste this pain. In the name of the One whose pain accomplished the ultimate redemptive purpose, amen."

RESOURCES

Books

1. Michael Card, *Sacred Sorrows: Reaching Out to God in the Lost Language of Lament* (NavPress, 2005).

2. Elisabeth Elliot, *Suffering Is Never for Nothing* (B & H Publishing Group, 2019).

3. Timothy Keller, *Walking with God through Pain and Suffering* (Penguin Books, 2013).

4. Alan Nelson, *Embracing Brokenness: How God Refines Us Through Life's Disappointments* (NavPress, 2002).

5. John Piper and Justin Taylor, *Suffering and the Sovereignty of God* (Crossway Books, 2006).

6. John Piper, *The Hidden Smile of God: The Fruit of Affliction in the Lives of John Bunyan, William Cowper, and David Brainerd* (Crossway Books, 2001).

7. David Powlison, *God's Grace in Your Suffering* (Crossway, 2018).

8. Vaneetha Risner, *The Scars That Have Shaped Me: How God Meets Us in Suffering* (Desiring God, 2016).

9. Joni Eareckson Tada, *Beside Bethesda: 31 Days Toward Deeper Healing* (NavPress, 2014).

10. Joni Eareckson Tada, *A Place of Healing: Wrestling with the Mysteries of Suffering, Pain, and God's Sovereignty* (David C. Cook, 2010).

11. Ann Voskamp, *The Broken Way* (Zondervan, 2016).

12. Mark Vroegop, *Dark Clouds, Deep Mercy: Discovering the Grace of Lament* (Crossway, 2019).

13. Nancy Leigh DeMoss Wolgemuth, *Brokenness, Surrender, Holiness* (Moody Press, 2008).

14. Philip Yancey, *Disappointment with God: Three Questions No One Asks Aloud*, 25th Anniversary Edition (Zondervan, 2015).

15. Philip Yancey, *The Question That Never Goes Away: Why?* (Zondervan, 2013).

16. Ravi Zacharias and Vince Vitale, *Why Suffering? Finding Meaning and Comfort When Life Doesn't Make Sense* (FaithWords, 2014).

Organizations & Websites
Joni & Friends

Joni & Friends (Joni Eareckson Tada) brings the Gospel of Christ and practical resources to people around the globe who are impacted by disability. This organization also equips Christ-honoring churches to evangelize and to disciple people in their communities who are affected by disability.

Chronic Joy (Chronic Illness Ministry)

Mission: Radical Hope. Compassionate Change. Equipping those affected by chronic physical and mental illness through community and education rooted in Jesus Christ.

Extensive resources provided in the areas of chronic illness, caregiving and mental illness. Blogs, books and more.

Broken Believers

Broken Believers (website and blog) is dedicated to serving *broken* Christians through a message of discipleship. Special attention is given to ministering to mental illnesses and other disabilities. Founded by Bryan Lowe. The center of this ministry is the blog.

Rest Ministries

This ministry offers support for persons with chronic illness or pain, and serves needs of their caregivers. *Rest Ministries* offers devotionals, online support groups and a blog. They are dedicated to serving *broken* Christians through a message of discipleship.

Life in Slow Motion

Blog and online courses for dealing with chronic pain, directed by Esther Smith, a licensed and biblical counselor. Their focus is "Chronic Pain and the Christian Life." Esther's short book is titled *But God, Wouldn't I Be More Useful to You If I Were Healthy?*

Broken but Priceless Ministries (with Erin Elizabeth Austin)

This is an interdenominational, non-profit Christian ministry that encourages individuals suffering with a chronic illness and serves their caregivers. Their mission is to help people with chronic illness see that even though their bodies are broken, they are priceless in God's eyes.

Their online magazine includes testimonies and reviews of resources that offer a biblically based hope. This ministry also maintains a blog.

ABOUT THE AUTHORS

 **Dr. Mark A. Smith** is President of Columbia International University, a growing university in South Carolina. He previously served as President of Ohio Christian University for 12 years, where he led a team of experts in growing the university from 380 to more than 4,700 students, and helped fund $30 million in facilities. He has served on the Board of Directors for the Association for Biblical Higher Education (ABHE) and Columbus 2020. He currently serves on the ELEOS Corporate Board. The governor of South Carolina recently appointed him to the South Carolina Commission of Higher Education. Dr. Smith has a B.A. from Hobe Sound Bible College, a M.S. from Northeastern State

University and graduated from West Virginia University with a Doctorate in Education Administration. Dr. Smith completed Harvard University's Institute of Educational Management for Executive Management. Dr. Smith and his wife, Debbie, have two children.

Terry Powell taught for 38 years in the Church Ministry program at Columbia International University. He earned his PhD from Trinity Evangelical Divinity School. For a total of twelve years, he served in both full-time and part-time capacities as an associate staff member of three churches. He is a licensed preacher in the Presbyterian Church of America (PCA). Terry has written or coauthored 19 books, including *Serve Strong: Biblical Encouragement to Sustain God's Servants* (Leafwood). He has taught courses or seminars in at least fifteen countries. He maintains a blog on depression and faith, **penetratingthedarkness.com**. Terry and his wife, Dolly, have two grown sons, a daughter by marriage, and a grandson.

OTHER BOOKS
BY THE AUTHORS

Mark Smith

Leading Change in Your World, **Larry Lindsay and Mark Smith**

This book presents an innovative change model predicated on the idea that world-changing leadership starts from the inside out. Readers examine valuable leadership strategies that will challenge them to become effective change agents.

Practical topics covered include, but aren't limited to:

- Changing the World—Who, Me?
- Collaborating with the Team

- Conceptualizing the Vision
- Developing a Strategic Plan
- Implementing, Monitoring, and Assessing Intended Results
- Overcoming Obstacles

In addition to insights gleaned from their own experience, the authors quote other experts on leadership, organizational behavior, change, and teamwork. Discover why a number of schools use this book as a text, and why Zig Ziglar said this about it: "Its purpose is to allow you to lead change, as opposed to letting change take you along with it."

To enhance one's study and application of the principles, the authors wrote a separate *Action Learning Guide*. The book and Guide are available online or at Wesleyan Publishers.

Leading Above and Beyond: Making Christ Known Through the Power of Biblical Leadership

Take Mark Smith's "30-day challenge" by prayerfully immersing yourself in this book for one month, one short chapter each day. Each leadership challenge or insight will make you a better leader in whatever role God has given you. Topics include, but aren't limited to:

- Leaders Lead with Character
- Leaders are Accountable
- Leaders Overcome Obstacles
- Leaders Develop Leaders

- Leaders Begin with Prayer
- Leaders Embrace Change
- Leaders Don't Take Shortcuts
- Leaders Build a Team

In each chapter, Dr. Smith employs Scripture. He also utilizes pertinent quotes from other leaders, past and present. Clarity and practicality describe these potent readings. Available at Amazon or from Columbia International University (www. ciu.edu).

Terry Powell

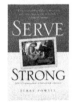

Serve Strong: Biblical Encouragement to Sustain God's Servants

Serve Strong (Leafwood, 2014) offers biblical insights to fuel the passion of vocational Christian leaders and serious volunteers. Discover truths that have sustained Terry for over 50 years of ministry.

- Bible promises pertinent to anyone who serves.
- How God uses pain, brokenness, weakness and delays to facilitate ministry fruitfulness.
- Reasons not to "lose heart" despite the fatigue, warfare and other pressures of ministry.
- How God defines "ministry success" differently than most people.
- Why our own abilities and experience are not adequate reasons for confidence.
- Stories from history, as well as contemporary anecdotes, that illustrate the biblical reassurances.

The late CIU president, missionary statesman and author Robertson McQuilkin said this about the book: "I can't remember reading a more powerful book of encouragement for pastors, missionaries, and Bible teachers. Well-written, fresh, penetrating."

You can order *Serve Strong* through bookstores or online sites such as Amazon.

Now That's a Good Question! How to Lead Quality Bible Discussions

A practical handbook for classroom Bible teachers of youth or adults, and small group leaders.

Learn how to:

- Create a group climate in which Bible discussions thrive.
- Ask observation, interpretation and application questions about your Bible passage or topic.
- Write original questions in a biblically and educationally sound manner.
- Prepare a sequential, start-to-finish Bible study plan.
- Expand and deepen the contributions of group members.
- Prevent or minimize problems such as monopolizers, tangents and a "pooling of ignorance."
- Cultivate a hospitable group atmosphere through numerous team-building ideas Terry provides.

"This is a book that delivers on its subtitle, *How to Lead Quality Bible Discussions*. Terry arms you with a weapons cache of knowledge, common mistakes to avoid, and an arsenal of ideas and templates. This is a small group masterpiece. It has quickly become one of the two top books that I recommend on facilitating group discussion."

Andrew Mason, Pastor, founder of SmallGroupChurches. com

Order this revised and expanded edition through Amazon books.

ENDNOTES

1   Ron Dunn, "The Ministry of Failure: Deuteronomy 8," Lifestyle Ministries, 2005. rondunn.com/ the-ministry-of-failure/.

2   James I. Packer, *Knowing God* (Downers Grove: InterVarsity Press, 1973), 226.

3   The author gleaned all quotes from Rob Hartman in a personal, face-to-face interview, Spring 2019.

4   The author gleaned the quote from Dr. Andre Rogers in a face-to-face interview, Spring 2019.

5   The author gleaned this quote from a tape of Ron Dunn's sermon, "The Ministry of Weakness," originally heard in 1975.

6   The author obtained all quotes from Craig Brown (chapters 8–9) through a telephone interview, Spring 2019.

7 From John Maxwell blog, "Are You Really Leading, or Are You Just Taking a Walk?" August 7, 2012.

8 The author obtained the quote from Elvin Weinmann by means of an email interview, Spring 2019.

9 As quoted by Bob Holmes, "CIU's Seventh President Takes the Reins," in *CIU Today* (Fall 2017), 17.

10 Scott Adams, as quoted in "CIU Growing with New Global Business & IT Center," *CIU Today* (Spring 2018), 19.

11 Mark Smith, as quoted in "News Conference: Partnership with Neighborhoods to Spur Economic Development," at www.ciu.edu, 3.

12 Steve Benjamin, as quoted in Melina Waldrop's "Columbia International Completes Property Purchases," in *Columbia Business Report* (May 7, 2019), 3.

13 Richard Day, *Bush Aglow: The Life Story of Dwight Lyman Moody, Commoner of Northfield* (Valley Forge: Judson Press, 1936), 9.

14 Charles Spurgeon, *The Greatest Fight in the World* (Shawnee, Kansas: Gideon House Books, 2016), 10.

15 Dallas Willard, "Spiritual Formation in Christ for the Whole Life and Whole Person," in *Vocatio*, Vol. 12, no. 2, (Spring 2001), 7.

16 Martin Luther, as found in "Martin Luther Quotes" at *A-Z Quotes* online.

17 Richard Foster, *Prayer: Finding the Heart's True Home* (San Francisco: Harper, 1992), from the chapter on "Petitionary Prayer," 179–190.

18 John Piper, *Desiring God: Meditations of a Christian Hedonist* (Sisters: Multnomah Books, 2011), 140, 144.

19 Charles Spurgeon, as quoted in John Piper's *Future Grace* (Sisters: Multnomah Books, 1995), 9.

20 From a *Family Circus* cartoon appearing in newspapers by syndication, by Bil Keane (Yes, he spelled his name with one "l"!).

21 Mark Vroegop, *Dark Clouds, Deep Mercy: Discovering the Grace of Lament* (Wheaton: Crossway, 2019), 21.

22 Nancy DeMoss Wolgemuth, *Brokenness, Surrender, Holiness* (Chicago: Moody Press, 2008), 42.

23 This analogy of "breaking a wild stallion" first appeared in Terry Powell's *Serve Strong: Biblical Encouragement to Sustain God's Servants* (Abilene: Leafwood Publishers, 2014), 103.

24 The author gleaned this quote from the Scottish novelist George MacDonald, in a novel read in the 1990s. He could not locate the specific book title from which he gleaned it.

25 Alan Nelson, *Embracing Brokenness: How God Refines Us Through Life's Disappointments* (Colorado Springs: NavPress, 2002), 18.

26 A form of this quote has been attributed to many authors and speakers, past and present. The earliest attribution I found was to St. Augustine of Hippo.

27 R.T. Kendall, *Total Forgiveness, Revised and Updated* (Lake Mary: Charisma House, 2007). See material in Chapter 2 of his book, "How to Know We Have Totally Forgiven," 49–76.

28 Marsha Hays, "Hidden in My Heart: Music to Soothe the Soul," a blog at her website: IWantThemToRemember. com.

29 From "Martin Luther Quotes About Music," *A-Z Quotes* online.

30 Marsha Hays, "Hidden in My Heart: Music to Soothe the Soul."

31 Michelle Bengtson, *Hope Prevails* (Grand Rapids: Revell, 2016), 17.

32 John Piper, *Future Grace* (Sisters: Multnomah Books, 1995), 38.

33 The author heard this statement in a "live" presentation by Bill Gothard during an "Institute in Basic Youth Conflicts" seminar in Chicago, Illinois (Spring 1972).

34 Warren Wiersbe, *The Strategy of Satan: How to Detect and Defeat Him* (Wheaton: Tyndale Publishers, 1979).

35 The author heard this quote from Stuart Briscoe during a chapel message at Wheaton College and Graduate School, April, 1972.

36 Vaneetha Risner, *The Scars That Have Shaped Me* (Minneapolis: Desiring God, 2016), 155.

37 D.A. Carson, *How Long, O Lord? Reflections on Suffering and Evil* (Grand Rapids: Baker Academic, 1990), 109.

38 Zack Eswine, *Spurgeon's Sorrows: Realistic Hope for Those Who Suffer from Depression* (Geanies House, Fearn, Ross-shire: Christian Focus Publications, 2014), 138.

39 Elisabeth Elliot, *Suffering Is Never for Nothing* (Nashville: B & H Publishing Group, 2019), 23.

40 Joni Eareckson Tada, *Beside Bethesda: 31 Days Toward Deeper Healing* (Colorado Springs: NavPress, 2014), 81.

41 Packer, *Knowing* God, 227.

42 Joni Eareckson Tada, *Beside Bethesda*, 168.

CPSIA information can be obtained
at www.ICGtesting.com
Printed in the USA
JSHW020225051120
9325JS00002B/111